C000260344

BEAUTIFUL
CORPORATIONS

BEAUTIFUL
CORPORATIONS

CORPORATE STYLE IN ACTION

Written by Paul Dickinson

Designed by Neil Svensen

FINANCIAL TIMES
Prentice Hall

London · New York · San Francisco · Toronto · Sydney
Tokyo · Singapore · Hong Kong · Cape Town · Madrid
Paris · Milan · Munich · Amsterdam

PEARSON EDUCATION LIMITED

Head Office:
Edinburgh Gate
Harlow CM20 2JE
Tel: +44 (0)1279 623623
Fax: +44 (0)1279 431059

London Office:
128 Long Acre
London WC2E 9AN
Tel: +44 (0)20 7447 2000
Fax: +44 (0)20 7240 5771
Website: www.business-minds.com

First published in Great Britain in 2000

ISBN 0 273 64233 2

British Library Cataloguing in Publication Data
A CIP catalogue record for this book can be obtained from the
British Library.

10 9 8 7 6 5 4 3 2 1

Typeset by Madark
Printed and bound in Great Britain by Redwood Books,
Trowbridge, Wiltshire

The Publishers' policy is to use paper manufactured from
sustainable forests.

ABOUT THE AUTHORS

Paul Dickinson is Director of Research at Rufus Leonard. Paul has a master's degree in Responsibility and Business Practice, is a fellow of the RSA, and director of the EYE Network and Diarymanager.com. Paul has been funded by companies including Intel - the world's largest computer company - to campaign for reduced CO_2 emissions. He has also written *Successful Web Sites*.

Neil Svensen is Managing Director at Rufus Leonard. Neil has a first degree in Graphic Design and has a design scholarship from IBM. His clients include Shell International, BT, Mercedes, Lloyds TSB and Royal Mail. Neil's work is in the permanent collection of the Victoria & Albert Museum. He has also written *The Knowledge Manager*.

CONTENTS

FOREWORD

Business dominates the global stage. It is faster, more creative and wealthier than governments, particularly the governments in developing nations who depend upon its expertise. Listen to the economists, and you get the sense that, if we just get out of the way of big business, an unregulated global economy will knit the peoples of the world together into a seamless quilt. In that world, workers earn decent wages, work in modern conditions, and spend their money on goods and services they only dreamed about before. In that world, human rights follow increasing prosperity, and nations are more and more reluctant to go to war with one another because they have too much at stake in each other's economy. In that world, multinational corporations are the driving force for the common good.

But multinationals are also the driving force in this world, where the flipside of globalisation is glaringly obvious: forced labour, sweatshops, children forced to work long hours, the poisoning of air, water and land, the dislocation of entire communities, brutal dictatorships, gross inequalities of wealth. Global planning institutions, like the World Bank, the IMF and especially the World Trade Organisation, are part of the problem. They ignore mounting evidence of a very real social catastrophe: poverty, not just economic and spiritual but also poverty of the imagination.

The reality is ugly. Paul Dickinson's antidote is obvious: beauty. If that sounds too glib to countenance, give his proposition some deeper consideration and it starts to make sense. I share his belief that business needs an aesthetic dimension to communicate its messages. Attention to aesthetics appeals to our finer instincts. So the more 'beauty' there is in business, the more it functions as a force for positive social change.

What Dickinson attempts to show is how this evolution is not a superficial process. As he so rightly points out, business has overtaken politics as the primary shaping force in society, which means consumers are 'voting' every time they flex their spending muscle, and that in turn makes the vigilante consumer into a powerful organism, capable, as we have seen, of humbling even the likes of Shell and Monsanto.

And how are businesses going to reach this consumer in the future? Dickinson would answer truth, beauty, goodness. Romantic? Perhaps. But there is real pragmatism here as well when he outlines the problems of identity management and the repercussions of 'values-free' business practices.

We are already rethinking our approach to the global role of business. The beautiful corporation is an honourable goal.

Anita Roddick, Chairperson,
The Body Shop International plc.

ACKNOWLEDGEMENTS

Firstly I must thank Neil Svensen who has been my teacher and friend for eleven years. As a designer and consultant of growing international repute, he would have written a better book, but instead was kind enough to fund me in the endeavour. Thanks also to Steve Howell and all my other colleagues at Rufus Leonard.

I must also thank the many great companies and individuals who have been kind enough to contribute to this book, Kevin Allfrey at Lloyds TSB, Mark Sands at ONdigital, IKEA, Shell, BT, Johnson & Johnson and many others.

Great thanks are due to my MSc tutors Gill Coleman, director of the New Academy of Business, and Professor Judi Marshall and Doctor Peter Reason of University of Bath School of Management.

Looking back, the fashion designer and cultural guru Katherine Hamnett taught me a great deal, Lynn Hall explained to me how the design industry worked, and with the late Chris Roberts, was kind enough to give me my first break.

Graeme LittleJohn, formerly of Kingsway College, was my one outstanding teacher of National Curriculum and earned his salary, in spades. Thank you Graeme.

Peter Ashman years ago took the time to explain why it is reasonable to be positive and optimistic about the modern world. Thank you Peter. Daniel Bernstein has always provided me with huge inspiration regarding the role of business in society. Thanks also to Hazel Henderson who has found a way out of the madness with her pioneering work. To Anita Roddick, for all she has done to dare to be different. Corporations will never be the same.

To Martin Polden, Maria Adebowale and Guy Dehn who are police in a lawless world, acting through Environmental Law Foundation and Public Concern at Work.

My thanks are also very much due to my publisher Pradeep Jethi, who encouraged me and suffered the unenviable task of converting my unfocused thinking into a semi-coherent whole.

Thanks to my Aunt Anne Dickinson whose abstemious character in life provided me with some independence following her death. To my parents and family who have been kind enough to give me an education and moral ambition, to accompany my innate immorality!

I am indebted also to Yolanda van den Steen who provided many insights in this book, and suggested the excellent title.

Special thanks to Charon Crowe, Sarah Thornton, Frances Lewis and Benn Tilby who worked very hard against bad deadlines.

Finally, to my business partners Lisa Honan and Jonny Shipp, who have given me freedom to write this. Thanks also to Steve Morris who created me as an author, and all the clients and suppliers who have taught me over the years.

Paul Dickinson

INTRODUCTION

Beautiful Corporations. OK, you might be thinking, what kind of a book is this?

You could be imagining that this is some kind of millennial styleguide on how you've got to wear a black polo neck and a pair of Wannabes if you're going to work in a 21st Century, 'right on', Kate Moss-style organisation, full of useful colour theory on what shade of red is most likely to soothe a prospect into the big sale. Right?

Wrong. This is not about external surface appearance or beauty, it's about what kind of organisations might very well dominate the next century, or beyond if you're feeling frisky.

The idea of *Beautiful Corporations* is a critical one. The time is perfect for this book to arrive. It truly is one of the most exciting and scariest times to be in business. Old rules really are crumbling. The certainty and orthodoxy of industry are being challenged by all manner of people, working in all manner of organisations. In such tricky times we need help to make sense of the confusion and complexity that many of us feel.

This book offers a map or a series of maps that many organisations will find useful in the new and unfamiliar business landscape they find themselves in. The reader will emerge from these pages with insights into good practices from today's beautiful corporations, a sense of how business can make a more comfortable bedfellow with the fragile earth, and an expanded understanding that corporate beauty is far from skin deep.

The businesses of tomorrow will be different, perhaps profoundly. They will have a certain beauty that comes from the core of the people running them. They will seek to move beyond the mere economic, short-term agendas of lining the pockets of a few, and seek to make meaning for the many.

They will see people not as human resources, but as human talents, aiming to realise potential, not control it. Beautiful corporations will touch the earth lightly, not using physical resources unnecessarily, but will use resources in new and more efficient ways. The corporation that will dominate tomorrow's business landscape will pursue the social as well as the financial agenda.

I believe the new business of business is making not products, brands or services, but making meaning. Making real meaning in the world.

The 'how to' is design. The new business of design can help beautiful corporations make meaning for people working in organisations, and the people those organisations serve.

This is the timely and valuable contribution this book is making. I implore you, the reader, to strive for creating beauty in your organisation, as Paul says: 'Corporations are now co-ordinating the world's consumption. Where material negligence or crass exploitation can be discerned, ugly corporations will have to reckon with assault from their more beautiful competitors. It is the beautiful corporations that will fight this good fight. And win!'

Sean Blair is establishing a new organisation, 'Nowhere' that creates profound innovation, for the businesses that will create the future, www.limitednowhere.com

Sean Blair, Design Director, Design Council; Director, Creative Catalyst, Limited Nowhere

CHAPTER ONE

Everywhere companies and their brands shout for our attention in the global language of design, and only the most memorable win.

SETTING THE SCENE

Everywhere companies and their brands shout for our attention in the global language of design, and only the most memorable win.

This book explains some of the strategies used by successful companies to manage their communications and offers advice and guidance on best practice.

Naturally there is more to success than simply looking good. In terms of meeting customers' needs, providing value for money and acting responsibly, companies actually have to be good.

Consumers, now expect to experience the pleasing sensations of style and beauty from the companies with which they choose to deal. The pressure on companies does not emanate from customers alone; employees, too, demand the flexibility in work conditions that technology now permits. Many knowledge workers, including the author of this book, would rather be on the beach. Increasingly we are demanding and receiving the benefits that secure our commitment to the enterprise.

In the new millennium, a positive attitude will be the prerequisite of survival, to be communicated in every available media – from corporate advertising and design to all written communications, as well as in the tone of voice used and the ergonomics of the workspace itself.

Unceasing lowering of prices or increasing of volumes cannot successfully maximise our happiness: we are not machines with an infinite capacity to consume. What makes us happy is style, beauty, a positive attitude and pleasing experiences. Neither the accountant nor the engineer can deliver these alone. Truly successful, sustainable businesses need to recognise the contribution of designers, architects, stylists and other specialists who can honour the inherent potential for growth and dignity in human beings. Saying that the purpose of business is profit is like saying the purpose of life is breathing.

About this book

This book will show how successful managers combine business practice with a certain style and thereby communicate a positive corporate attitude to gain sustainable competitive advantage. The disciplines discussed are explained through case studies that show best practice in the use of design.

The universal concept of beauty provides a way for us to study these issues. The dictionary defines beauty as 'delighting the senses and pleasing the mind'. This book rejects any particular overarching philosophy of business. Instead it will demonstrate that the correct route towards fulfilling the potential for human happiness is to be found in the way things are done as much as what is done.

Many experienced managers in industry will read the title of this book and think, 'It's the bottom line that counts, that's what is beautiful'. It may surprise them to know that beauty – a certain style – adds value to the enterprise on the bottom line. To act without some semblance of style is commercial suicide. Humans respond to humanity and intelligence with attraction, and that results in sales.

We all want to live in a beautiful world, but economic development sometimes destroys more than it creates. The big idea in the twenty-first century is this: if you and your company are not part of the solution, you are part of the problem.

If you are not part of the solution, you are part of the problem.

This book will show how all these requirements converge in the world's greatest companies to create the style of the successful – the beautiful – corporations. The terms 'corporate identity' and 'brand' will be used somewhat interchangeably. Brands usually refer to products and corporate identity to companies, but organisations such as Shell, IBM and Coca-Cola could be described as having both corporate and product brands.

It is my belief that if globalisation is to be justified it must represent an aggregation up to a higher plane of aesthetics, rather than a drive down to the lowest common denominator. That may require more diversity, rather than less.

There is obviously much more to the achievement of profits than design style alone, and this makes establishing a direct, immediate link between excellence in design and profits rather difficult to establish. There are, however, notable exceptions, such as the new Apple iMac.

Poor products and poor communications are a visual indicator of company ugliness. It is the visual design of products, communications etc. that reflects the heart of invisible design shown in processes, culture etc.

The success of the iMac is an example of how an enormous amount of money can be made by simply doing something differently. Apple's London-born design director, Jonathan Ive, is only in his early thirties, but he has created many millions of dollars of value for Apple stockholders, and helped relaunch the company with some beautiful, innovative products.

Car design is an area where most of us enjoy the work of some of the world's greatest designers. Car manufacturers are eager to promote their corporate brands rather than the name of any individual, so car designers are usually restricted under contract from letting anyone know who they are. But our heads often turn when we see their work. In the UK we spend around £22 billion annually on cars, and aggregate global sales of the main car companies are spectacular. To see the peak of product design, look at cars.

There was once an excellent advertisement for a Mercedes sports car that showed this principal in action. Featuring a large photograph of the car, the slogan simply said: 'It's better than it looks.'

What is corporate style?

It has been said that if a person has style, it is something they never think about. The implication here is that style is an intrinsic characteristic that cannot be acquired. Like physical beauty, style is a positive attribute that we look for in those we encounter. We like it when we see it.

It is this acknowledgement that style is intrinsic that causes us to link it to corporate attitude, where issues such as integrity and honesty are prerequisites for success.

Not a corporate man

Some business theorists led by Thomas Frank, author of *The Conquest of Cool*, have suggested that the idea of 'cool', which emerged in the 1960s, has been appropriated as the official style of our business civilisation. Originally, the cool symbolised by James Dean and Jimmy Hendrix was a revolt against the existing order and it was revered as the next, better iteration of our society's development. However, at this political juncture, famously described as 'the end of history' by Francis Fukuyama (1992), there is nothing new ahead except bigger companies with more power. They will perhaps provide for both the mainstream and its alternative. In Frank's words:

The over-arching facts of economic life are that the society we live in is exploitative and joyless, but it [corporate cool] also offers us this ready-made opposition that you can buy off the rack. Globalisation and the triumph of markets worldwide is resulting in this sort of conflict between the 'hip' and the 'square'. This conflict is replacing older social conflicts like those between the workers and owners. That is the genius of this ideology, the sort of bogus conflict between hip and square is all over the world now, it is the international language of advertising.

Such complex concepts as 'cool' were first communicated and applied to brands and corporations through advertising. It has been suggested that Volkswagen first established its credentials as a cool company through previously unheard-of ironic advertising in the 1960s. This communicated that the brand had humanity and wit, something many Japanese car manufacturers would love to project.

The fact is that even the greatest corporations cannot make money from creating and selling art, or encouraging activities with cult followings such as snowboarding or skateboarding. Even with their billions of dollars they cannot lead youth culture or inspire love or affection, which means that a great proportion of human ingenuity and invention will perpetually lie outside their capabilities. They constantly try to acquire it. But the gentrification of this idiosyncrasy kills it. As Frank has said: 'The wolf of capitalism is perpetually chasing the cool sheep.'

The American media analyst Sara Vowell describes cool as comprising two essential components: a sense of justice and a sense of humour. When you know what justice is it means you have a heart, and when you have a sense of humour it means you have a brain. This is entirely consistent with Darwinian theories of attractiveness.

Vowell believes that in today's world caring is the brave thing and it communicates authenticity. Genuineness is important because you can tell when an organisation is lying to you. Trust is the key element in generating social capital.

There is a real need for integrity in the development of an organisation's culture. Companies including Nike, Microsoft and Apple have attracted criticism because of the gap between their projection of reality and the reality of the underlying company. Achieving a corporate reputation embracing honesty and integrity will never be easy.

This concept of integrity lies at the heart of a successful enterprise. A company such as Pizza Express offers good food, at a reasonable price, in a nice atmosphere. As it has grown it has continued to express the original owner's vision. Delivery of this kind of consistency and fidelity to the underlying spur of business is a form of integrity. Even if such a company is later purchased by a vast conglomerate, if it is a strong business with a strong ethic, it should be able to retain its integrity.

Citroên cars have always had a certain style and appeal. Interestingly this often reflects from the product to the customer and then back to the product. The lifestyle legend associated with the Citroên 2CV is a good example of this.

Although it can be easy to tire of what the great media analyst Marshall McLuhan called the 'ceaseless barrage of advertising messages which daily assault us' (McLuhan, 1994), in the UK we are lucky. The UK advertising industry is spectacularly innovative and stimulating. Germaine Greer has described marketing as the great cultural phenomenon of our times. This challenging statement comes at a time when leading figures in the arts are rejecting concepts such as 'cool Britannia' and a perceived 'dumbing down' of culture.

It is up to the corporations to be aware of the issues. Advertising will be public art or sinister exploitation, depending on the capacity for companies to act with taste, a developed aesthetic sense, responsibility and intelligence.

In the words of David Korten in his terrifying book, *When Corporations Rule the World:*

When control of our cultural symbols passes to corporations, we are essentially yielding to them the power to define who we are. Instead of being Americans, Norwegians, Egyptians, Filipinos, or Mexicans, we become simply members of the 'Pepsi generation', detached from place and any meaning other than those a corporation finds it profitable to confer on us.

This is the dark side and we must avoid it.

What is creativity in design?

Throughout this book I avoid using the word 'creativity' to describe artists working in the communications industry. Because there are billions of neurones in the brain, every single human thought from every human, every second, is completely different to all others. It follows from this premise that everyone is exactly equally 'creative', and what people call the 'creative' process is a far more complex area involving high- and low-quality output. This in turn raises the question, from whose perspective?

In one sense the word 'creative' is lazy shorthand for a series of complex concepts. The same charge could also be made of the word 'brand'. For this reason I will try and break these terms down into their underlying meaning.

Why beauty?

The world is enjoying unprecedented wealth, our technology is fantastically advanced and progress is accelerating. However, we live in a time of great human suffering and a looming environmental crisis. Many pressure groups argue that global commerce has dislocated hundreds of millions of people. They say that the wealth we enjoy is partially the result of externalising our costs of production to the world's poorest nations.

These issues will not go away. We all have an absolute, unshirkable responsibility to ensure the world we are creating for our children is beautiful.

We all have a responsibility to create a beautiful world.

I believe that the underlying concept of beauty can be explained in a technical sense. This book is written from an atheist, Darwinist perspective. It is possible to see millions of examples of the great theory of evolution, some obvious and others less so. For example, I believe the global obsession with sports news and the relative performance of our athletes, our team or our country in sport is the inheritance of ten thousand generations of warlike, communicative mammals, eager to learn about the key survival skills of war.

Within the Darwinist framework, the concept of beauty, as applied to attraction between the sexes, is simple. Typically, fit and healthy people without deformities will be identified by prospective suitors as the most desirable partners for making babies, because they maximise the chances of survival of their offspring and the species.

But how does this simple conception of beauty apply to a beautiful sunset, a poem, painting or opera – or to a corporation? Underpinning our sense of attraction is a basic set of instincts that is drawn towards the 'good' and rejects the 'bad'. In this context, good and bad are simplistic terms used to describe presentation; they are not philosophical positions. However, they serve to illustrate the point.

So, to give an extreme example, in the 1930s the Nazis emerged under the fiendishly clever designer, Albert Speer, as the most visually arresting, unified and thereby seemingly coherent political organisation in Germany. Our animalistic instincts perceive unity, visual consistency and quality in communications as commensurate with order, which we believe to be capable and competent, and this translates into attraction.

In business, it is this attraction that fuels transactions and profits. But we should not worry too much that the new super global brands and corporations are riding on the back of a modern communications discipline whose first major exponents were the Nazis. Nature has equipped us with instincts that can, eventually, sniff out Nazis.

Let us look at beauty in a sunset, poem, painting or opera. When we see the sunset, with its 'glorious overhanging canopy, fretted with golden fire' as Hamlet said, it is a fairly good sign that the climate is okay to rest; or perhaps to stay to try and grow crops. The process of natural selection has taught us to stop and stay with beauty. The sea calls us for the same reason. Those that were attracted to living by the sea, with all its food sources, survived. Those that went back inland often died. That is why many of us love the sea. It is an instinct. Beauty provides an instinctive reference to the genetic essence of life purpose.

Instinctive attraction

In an opera, painting or poem we perceive other human consciousness, and actually experience it directly. These art forms can move us emotionally and we enjoy this. The meaning of art is to communicate actual living experiences directly, not a description of them that we need to interpret, but the real thing. Good art 'records' how the artist felt and plays it back to us.

Decoration is the celebration of matter

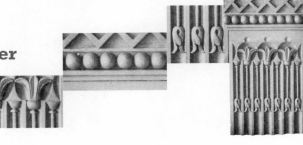

Nature is a hard taskmaster and does not reward us for spending our time with idiots. In actual fact, over millions of years, those that did like spending time interacting with idiots all died. A pre-programmed recognition of coherence and quality in logic has been developed in our minds and we use it to sift external stimuli. So after thousands of generations of natural selection, what do we, the ones that survived, really like? We love the intelligence and ingenuity of life. Over time our instincts inform us of the nihilistic terrors of Nazism, even if the Fascists do communicate a superficial visual coherence. In the final analysis, our intelligence establishes the underlying attitude of an organisation and can ascertain at the most instinctive level if it is 'pro life'.

From the Darwinist perspective, life is the cause of all perceived order. What defines life over chaos is replicating order; what defines intelligence over randomness is ordered systems of thinking.

Our living experience creates a perception of the external world. It generates the philosophical concept of order and applies it to what we see, hear, touch and smell. The defining characteristic of this order that emerges from chaos is replication. That is what defines life over randomness.

A great poem uses the ordered protocols of the written word to evoke a recognisable reality – love, longing, terror or some other emotion are summoned up by the imagery. So it is with painting and music.

And for corporations? This book will make the radical case that human attraction to order, replication and the intelligence required for survival are fundamental to the way consumers perceive corporations. As corporations have grown in stature, the way they act and communicate, their attitude and style, is what makes them winners or losers.

As a communications consultant I have spent many happy but frustrating years with colleagues trying to find meaningful product differentiation between one bank and another, one petrol retailer and another, and so on across all industry sectors. For 99 per cent of the time there simply is nothing to choose between the two. That is about to change forever. The sustainability crisis, climate change and numerous other limitations to growth in physical production are about to arrive: not as single spies but in battalions. Business can and will have to address this crisis. It represents both threat and opportunity.

This is the central idea behind the concept of 'sustainability product marketing' introduced in Chapter 5.

Beauty in the marketplace

The fashion and cosmetics industry, along with many others, draw upon human physical beauty in all their communications. Talent scouts with undefinable, infinitely complex criteria scour the world for the next Kate Moss supermodel. At the same time millions of beautiful young people apply to join the modelling industry. Throughout history beauty has been celebrated. And although today's near-anorexic catwalk waifs may seem to have not much to do with health and fitness, it is the genetic 'truth' of Darwinian natural selection that is manipulated to power sales of Calvin Klein products such as CK One and Eternity. Beauty sells.

In fact, the optimum physical expression of beauty suggested by 'survival of the fittest' may be replaced by the 'unnatural selection' of editors in the communications and fashion industries who create stereotypes that subvert conventional biological beauty-preference development.

Just as some languages in equatorial regions have no word for snow, because the population has never encountered it, so it is with aesthetics. The dominant organisations employing the power of artists to promote their interests control in many ways the very vocabulary of thought. The power of potential censorship exercised by aesthetic arbiters cannot be overestimated. The designer and artist Anno Mitchell examined the development of Nazi propaganda in occupied countries in her 1994 study *Heroism, Masochism and the Libidinal Economy of National Socialist Ethics*. She describes how the first thing the Nazis did after invasion was to take control of the arts policy in subjugated states.

The situation has changed somewhat since the dawn of the era of mass communication. But it can be argued that the global dream factory of Hollywood, armed and guarded by Coca-Cola, Disney, McDonald's and their like, is manifesting a similarly constricting effect on modern thought. For example, there has been a compression of the galaxy of experiences: eating may be limited to McDonald's, or clothing to Nike. There is a reduction in the diversity of language. This process is analogous to the constriction of words into 'Newspeak' that George Orwell outlined in his terrifying novel *1984*.

The process also occurs in politics, with consequences that emanate from the corporate centres of power and wealth in the industrialised world out to all mankind. The homogenising orthodoxy that blinkers us is a result of excessive amplification of any particular perspective; it is a consequence of the huge 'mindshare' enjoyed by successful modern brands. Globalisation through corporate capitalist culture has caused this. How we respond to it is a key theme of our age.

How we respond to globalisation is a key theme of our age.

Corporate consciousness

Charles Handy (1998) has observed that corporations can cheat death and live forever. Arie de Geus has written a fascinating study of this issue in his book *The Living Company*.

The tendency to anthropomorphise the corporation is well established amongst the business elite. Technology is a key driver of the unification of corporate intelligence. In the words of Bill Gates in his new book, *Business @ the Speed of Thought*:

To function in the digital age, we have developed a new digital infrastructure. It's like the human nervous system. The biological nervous system triggers your reflexes so that you can react quickly to danger or need. It gives you the information you need as you ponder issues and make choices. You're alert to the most important things, and your nervous system blocks out information that isn't important.

Companies need to have that same kind of nervous system: the same ability to run smoothly and efficiently; to respond quickly to emergencies and opportunities; to quickly get valuable information to the people in the company who need it; the ability to make decisions quickly and interact with customers.

As our great corporations mutate into living entities, the new science of corporate intelligence will manifest itself more profoundly. To quote Gates' intriguing book again:

To begin creating a digital nervous system, you should first develop an ideal picture of the information you need to run your business and to understand your markets and your competitors. Think hard about the facts that are actionable for your company. Develop a list of questions to which the answers would change your actions. Then demand that your information systems provide those answers. If your current system won't, you need to develop one that will – one or more of your competitors will.

In a telling revelation on the emergence of corporate consciousness, Gates goes on:

You know you have built an excellent digital nervous system when information flows through your organisation as quickly and naturally as thought in a human being, and when you can use technology to marshal and co-ordinate teams of people as quickly as you can focus an individual on an issue. It's business at the speed of thought.

The Internet is the protocol that has emerged to govern computer interaction at the beginning of the twenty-first century, but the inevitable trend was discernible far earlier. It was Sun Microsystems which coined the enigmatic but ultimately profound phrase 'the network is the computer'™ as early as 1991, well before the Internet permeated the public consciousness.

When reviewing the Internet revolution for the *Financial Times*, Christopher Price (18 March 1999) observed: 'The value of a company's physical assets are giving way to the intangible value inherent in its brands, research and development, consumer relationships and market knowledge.'

This book is about the next great phase in capitalist development. Giant companies are beginning to divorce their wealth, their talent, and perhaps even – to borrow a religious word – their souls, from physical manifestations. This process has been going on for a long time. Spectacular brand valuations from RHM (£600m) and Guinness (£1.7bn) began to appear on balance sheets almost ten years ago. These huge abstract 'intangible' assets have greatly exercised the minds of auditors.

In the new millennium it will be the corporate attitude – the essence – that will favour certain corporations over others. And this trend will become increasingly relevant as the sustainability crisis emerges into the public consciousness.

Past, present, future

Throughout history there have been great corporations. Some people include the church and the army amongst their number. But in this book I concentrate only on profit-orientated commercial organisations. Which is of course just about all any business has ever been, dating back to when we lived in caves.

But there is something altogether different about the modern large-scale corporate enterprise. Richard Barnett and Ronald Muller (1974) have described the process eloquently:

The US economy has dominated the American century

The men who run global corporations are the first in history with the organisation, technology, money, and ideology to make a credible try at managing the world as an integrated economic unit. What they are demanding in essence is the right to transcend the nation-state and in the process, transform it.

As David Korten (1995) puts it:

There is no conspiracy, though in practical terms, the consequences are much as if there were. Unlike real people ... corporations are able to grow ... amassing power indefinitely. Eventually that power evolves beyond the ability of any mere human to control.

This is where we are today.

Is this new order an anti-democratic tendency? Perhaps. Or perhaps the exact reverse. Malcolm McIntosh (1998), European Director of the Council on Economic Priorities, has described it with supreme elegance:

Choice. The foundation of a successful market economy. The bedrock of personal citizenship. I shop therefore I am! I choose therefore I have freedom. When I shop I vote. I vote for a certain sort of society, local and global, by choosing organic fair-trade coffee. In making my choice I hope that as an informed member of society I am minimising my environmental impact, contributing to a change in farming practice and significantly aiding economic and social development locally and globally.

Have we voted for the corporations that run the economic engine of our world, at a million tills, on a billion occasions, in a hundred countries? Or perhaps, more frighteningly, is any human really any longer in charge of the industrial process? Have we surrendered our democratic and political will to a system, to a process, to a market? The answer to that question is probably the heart of modern politics. This book will not attempt to answer it. But it will introduce the characters in this great play of human history and suggest a way forward.

Is any human in charge of the industrial process?

It will show what a modern corporation looks like – literally – and show how human ingenuity has amalgamated into a new global style. Perhaps the end of history, perhaps a new world order.

Corporations making history

History is full of events of little or no significance to future generations. But there are exceptions. The explosion of organisation, scientific discovery and communication, backed by military strength that characterised the Roman Empire, has many echoes today. University buildings, state monuments and religious works feature Latin text. Interestingly, Hitler and the Nazis closely imitated much of the symbolism and heraldry of the Roman Empire for their short-lived, putative world government.

Major advances in society – which in recent years have been predominantly technological – have the immediate effect of validating in the public consciousness the authority of the political system that prevailed at the time of their introduction.

At any juncture of significant scientific advance the prevailing governing authority is happy to be associated with the new achievements. For example, Lenin described communism as 'Soviet power plus the electrification of the whole country' (Lenin, 1920). Companies in 1928 such as Radio, Wright Aero, Ford and American Telegraph and Telephone validated the craze for speculation which precipitated the crash through the genuine offer of technologies that were destined to transform the world.

The Nazis applied the industrial techniques of Henry Ford to aircraft production and used them to develop aircraft fleets that exceeded 1,000 for the first time, promising to 'rub out' UK cities. They almost did.

In our age, associations are increasingly made between achievements and corporations. The global miracle of combining refrigeration, guaranteed safe-to-drink fluids and caffeine for millions of people, equates to Coca-Cola. For others the profound magic of travel by air, at hundreds of miles per hour, in near perfect safety, means Boeing. The numerous miracles of modern computing belong not to Babbage, the computer's inventor, but to Cisco, Intel and IBM.

In a subtle, mysterious but profound way, these brands have slowly come to define our age, our capabilities and the essence of human achievement. What this means in practical terms is an increasing recognition on the part of the general public for a diminished role for government. Following the privatisation revolution that has gripped the world, government physically undertakes less and less. There is perhaps a 'responsibility deficit' in society that urgently needs addressing. This issue is one of the themes in the MSc in Responsibility and Business Practice run jointly by the University of Bath and the New Academy of Business. I would recommend the course to any reader.

Society goes on changing faster and faster at the hands of corporations. Modern marketing up until now has been designed to ensure that consumers buy products. Corporations have been fairly exclusively concerned with maximising returns to shareholders. Through the increasingly multifaceted array of activities that has been made possible by the explosion of technology, corporations have advanced the speed of the world to such a fever pitch that it is about to suffer ecological catastrophe. And governments have now probably withered to such an extent that they cannot help. So the runaway train is still rolling down the hill faster and faster until it hits the buffers and we are all destroyed.

Professor Judi Marshall of the University of Bath School of Management calls this a crisis of 'systemic proportions'. The system itself is faulty.

This crisis provides a tremendous commercial opportunity. But unlike Churchill, whose call to arms promised nothing more than blood, pain, tears and sweat, this challenge promises higher margins, increased market share and sustainable profits.

It is useful to try to see what is going on in the three interconnected agents of this revolution, namely technology, globalisation and the environmental crisis.

Technology

The typesetting industry has disappeared, along with most filing clerks, typists and numerous other seemingly essential trades in the world. Time spent on-line is rapidly approaching time spent watching television in our households. Data has already overtaken voice conversation as the main traffic on most telephone networks. The speed of this change and the vast potential of the network development mean there is no reason at all to believe the process will slow down – quite the reverse in fact.

Use of mobile telephones has exploded to 300 million – one in twenty of all humans. As in other trends in computing and communications, a network effect is in operation, referred to as Metcalf's law. Each new user of any system increases the utility applying to all the users.

All this technology does not come cheap. The seemingly unending boom in technology spending can largely explain the North American economic miracle. Perhaps the Reagan Administration's massive investment in high-technology weapons had more practical spin-offs than the rise of Boris Yeltsin.

Perhaps that happy combination of defence research fuelling technological innovation could point the way forward. Charles Handy (1998) has suggested optimistically that:

'We could, for instance, define the environment as the new target for defence expenditure, fending off our own deterioration.'

Globalisation

Globalisation is the full expression of the basic human instinct to trade. The unprecedented level of international trade prevailing today is a consequence of many factors, including the near global adoption of capitalist commercial systems, the development of international agreements, rising disposable incomes in the industrialised economies, and above all, technology.

Affordable air transport has massively increased tourism, computers have facilitated increased logistical capability and card organisations such as Visa have globalised money.

Globalisation is the full expression of the instinct to trade.

Globalisation is the word on most social scientists' lips. The 1999 Reith lectures by Professor Anthony Giddens, Director of the London School of Economics, were on the subject of the 'Runaway world', examining the role of global companies in both economic and political terms. Transnational corporations are the new agents of commerce and industry.

Their size brings them increased purchasing power and therefore lower priced goods.

This self-reinforcing trend increases their scale and makes them larger still. Whilst there will be many areas of commercial development that are not suited to global companies, what they can take, they will. They have streamlined IT and finance. They can write off research and development against vast turnover, and can source production from the lowest-cost manufacturer. There is no reason to believe the trend towards globalisation will reverse. It will accelerate.

Edward Luce (23 March 1999) wrote in the *Financial Times* that:

The logic of economic globalisation has resulted in a split between a class of increasingly liquid and international blue-chip stocks and derivatives on the one hand, and a more domestic category of small cap stocks and derivatives instruments on the other. The outperformance of the S & P 500 against the Russell 2000 index of smaller cap stocks, or the FTSE 250 against the FTSE Small Cap Index, over the past three years is testimony to the growing sway of cross-border investors who seem to have neither the time nor the patience to invest their cash in smaller equities.

At the 1999 World Economic Forum conference in Davos, Switzerland, on the subject of 'Responsible Globality, Managing the Impact of Globalisation', the German President Roman Herzog spoke of the need for a 'global economy with a human face. Globality forces us to seek not only a new financial and economic order but also a world social order'.

The Times (3 March 1999) commented on the conference:

In a world in which the state is shrinking and corporations are going global as nations cannot, executives have to take on some of the responsibilities traditionally the preserve of politicians if the forum's stated aim of 'Improving The State Of The World' is to be addressed.

From every perspective of the business world comes a concern at the practical impact of globalisation. Jon Corzine, co-chairman of Goldman Sachs & Co., said at Davos: 'Globalisation needs to have a heart if it's going to be triumphant and not just dominant . . . It must be seen as a popular crusade that benefits every sector of society.'

Jeffrey Garten (*Business Week*, 25 January 1999), Dean of the Yale School of Management and former Under Secretary of Commerce in the Clinton Administration, has eloquently expressed the dilemma:

Defence contractors such as Lockheed Martin, the result of a 1995 merger, have successfully pushed for NATO expansion and for related military sales to Poland, the Czech Republic and others. Combined entities such as Boeing-McDonnell Douglas will tighten their already formidable grip on US trade policy. Companies like Exxon-Mobil Corp. will deal with oil-producing countries almost as equals, conducting the most powerful private diplomacy since the British East India Company wielded near-sovereign clout throughout Asia.

Clare Short (UK Government Press Release 22 October 1999), Minister for Overseas Development, said: 'My view is that globalisation is as big a historical shift as the move from feudalism to industrialisation. It means we have to find ways of making sure capital serves people and not the other way round.'

Organisations have been set up to address these issues, such as the Joint Forum of Indian People Against Globalisation (Jafip), comprising some 55 member groups of farm and labourers' unions and representing millions of members. Jafip has campaigned for India to leave the World Trade Organisation (WTO), an engine of globalisation. It has protested in response to stark events such as the 450 suicides of peasant farmers in two states that were alleged to be in response to WTO policies such as the removal of import tariffs on edible oils. Spokesperson Medha Patkar (*Guardian*, 27 January 1999) has said:

All living systems are in decline

'So-called modern technology has worked against the natural resource-based community, undermining self-reliance and creating vulnerability through dependency on pesticides and fertilisers, and on the market.'

In our own culture, too, there is a challenging interface, particularly in the service industries, between the hard economics of the market pushing wages down to the minimum, and the humanity we want to see society fostering as we strive to improve the livelihood of all individuals.

John Maynard Keynes (1933) said that it is better to export recipes than cakes. In this farsighted analysis he predicted both the infinite potential for the exchange of media, but also the threats of globalisation:

Ideas, knowledge, art, hospitality, travel – these are the things which should of their nature be international. But let goods be home spun wherever it is reasonably and conveniently possible, and above all, let finance be primarily national.

The environmental crisis

We should not be paralysed by guilt or depression as a result of this impending doom. It is not your fault or mine. But we can make a fortune fixing it. In fact, quite soon the only way to make money will be to contribute to the solution of a problem. And the bigger and more serious the problem, the faster and fatter the profits will be.

Living, thinking and doing sustainable business means first of all an acknowledgement that the entire ecosystem is in jeopardy. It is, but we must learn to accept that fact fundamentally. As the eminent environmentalist, Paul Hawken, author of *The Ecology of Commerce*, has commented: 'All living systems are in decline.'

From this realisation, everything else follows as night follows day.

40 million acres of forest, an area roughly the size of Nepal, are destroyed each year. These numbers seem impossible to grasp, but just consider what an acre really is and what a million really means.

The environmental problem that threatens us most directly is climate change. It destroys the self-regulating temperature mechanism of the Earth. The distinguished scientist James Lovelock demonstrated many years ago that our planet has a self-regulating climate system. It is in no way fantastic that nature has produced a self-regulating temperature system for the earth. For example, you have one in your body.

The greatest environmental problem is climate change.

In essence, the environmental crisis can be best understood by the following simple test. Look around you: in the supermarket, at the shopping centre, in the traffic. There are currently six billion humans on spaceship Earth. Six hundred million have cars. Human use of technology results in the emission of six billion tons of CO_2 into the atmosphere each year. Do you think our life support system can support all this consumption?

The financial system

The three areas of change described above are interwoven with our idolisation of the simplistic science of economics. The measurement of Gross National Product (GNP) has been described by Maralyn Waring, the former Head of Public Accounts for the New Zealand Government as 'chronically malevolent'. Under this system, oil spills and other catastrophes increase GNP, while all forms of domestic work, care for the disadvantaged and other acts of compassion are unmeasured. Politicians' exclusive focus on achieving growth in GNP leads to expanding the money-measured side of society to the detriment of all others.

However, the absolutely fatal flaw with GNP is what it does not measure. It does measure each country's total 'sales', like a profit and loss account, although it counts all sales as profit. The terrifying reality is that there is no accompanying balance sheet. So the GNP figure offers us an ultimately one-dimensional perspective on our financial position. In accountancy jargon, we are liquidating our environmental assets for nothing more than a false statement of profit.

Is there really a problem?

On 5 March 1999 the US State Department reported that air temperatures were the hottest in 500 years and tropical sea-surface temperatures were the highest in modern record, which caused the largest death of coral reefs ever witnessed. UK Environment Minister Michael Meacher has described the impending catastrophe of climate change as 'the greatest challenge in human history'.

In his book *The Second World War*, Winston Churchill explains how he was asked by President Roosevelt the question: 'What should we call the war?' He wrote as follows: 'I answered without a moment's hesitation: "the unnecessary war". There never was a war more easy to stop than the one which has just wrecked what was left of the world from the previous struggle.'

Within this bleak context, I believe it is certain that the supreme power of markets and corporations will focus to ensure catastrophe is avoided.

CHAPTER TWO

The Coke bottle is a voluptuous design of genius by one of the greatest of all corporate designers, Raymond Loewy. Nothing after it will have the same impact.

THE ROLE AND IMPACT OF DESIGN

We have all grown up under a ceaseless hail of shrieking advertising messages. In response to this we have learnt – at the most fundamental, subconscious level – to filter out only what we want from the barrage. And the result is that we notice only those communications with a style that merits attention, only those that chime with our inner sensibilities regarding beauty and truth. Only the beautiful survive.

So many different and attractive concepts can be communicated in a simple design. For example, the Sapporo beer can arrived in the market with a classic, bulbous, metallic, industrial and minimalist feeling. These associations came as a welcome breath of fresh air for many beer drinkers who had been depressed by tawdry beer cans.

Another aspect of beauty in design is an anthropomorphic tendency. Examples include the VW Beetle, Porsche cars and the Philip Starck spider lemon squeezer. Starck has said the squeezer is not for lemons, but rather something for a newly married man to talk about with his mother-in-law.

The Coke bottle is a voluptuous design of genius by one of the greatest of all corporate designers, Raymond Loewy. Nothing after it will have the same impact; certainly not the attempt by Virgin to achieve the same through the 'Pammy' bottle.

Excellence in design

Consider these two views on excellence. Picasso suggested it is not hard to do good art. 'What is hard is to be in the right frame of mind to do good art.' John Wanamaker (1999) said: 'Half my advertising is useless, but I have no way of knowing which half.'

The design process is about leveraging the talent of an exceptional few, not the mucking in of the many. All too frequently in my career clients have told me they need a new design because the old one 'looks dated'. Part of me has a strong instinct to reject such a criticism. What they have is often not 'dated', rather I believe the problem is that they commissioned shoddy design in the first place. When corporations slavishly struggle to follow fashions they often just reveal themselves as vapid and weak. As the fashion designer Katharine Hamnett has said, nothing goes out of fashion like fashion. But look at the Shell logo designed by Raymond Loewy, or at the Concord airliner. These designs still look new today.

A general contemporary perception of 'design' might be the quality and co-ordination of aesthetic considerations as applied to commercial activity. The attention to detail to be found in every aspect of a typical Conran restaurant provides a modern working example of the meaning of design.

In this sense, design is about both the look and feel of a company. Successful designers aspire to improve both the intrinsic character of an organisation and all of its manifestations.

What this means for the business community is that you cannot simply hire a few designers and expect the magic to happen. Successful design companies have developed very sophisticated environments in which talented designers can feed off each other and the outside world.

Diesel, the highly successful fashion house, sends its designers on expensive world tours to draw from cultural diversity in a self-directed odyssey. The best design companies hold on to their people by both acknowledging and encouraging activities beyond the founding company.

Technology is also changing and sharpening the environment. In the new media economy it is easy to know exactly what percentage of your advertising is effective. One could even argue that advertising is the wrong term to use for what used to be called advertisements. In the hypertext world every advertisement is a shop.

In the hypertext world every advertisement is a shop.

The Design Council experience

An interview with Sean Blair, Design Director of the Design Council, highlighted his ideas on excellence on design:

Thinking about the word 'style' I think of all the different groups who use it. Manufacturers on Tyneside, high street banks, the Design Council, everyone really, and each is different.

Style has business benefits. The word style has a bad name. To call someone a 'stylist' is a good cocktail party insult. I have to re-frame what I think style is. It gives a sense of reassurance of the brand values of an organisation. A perception of the brand values.

What are brand values?
Either the conscious (preferably) or unconscious values that you wish to portray to the world. A combination of emotive values and researched business processes. At the Design Council we know what people should think about when they think of us. Our brand values are: 'collaborative, innovative, effective, knowledgeable, authoritative'.

These brand values are brought to life in the production of a communication; during the process we would try and make sure that those involved with the project understand the brand values.

We want to make sure concepts put to us are 'on brand'. Do they have the appropriate level of innovation? Are they authoritative? Do they suggest we are knowledgeable?

In this interview, are we collaborating? Was I knowledgeable? Was I authoritative? And although it sounds odd, you also need to ask whether a person is 'on brand'.

When we interview people for jobs we ask these questions; we look for the embedded cultural level of our brand values. So it is about basic processes but also culture. And it is up to all of us to guard these values, to live the values.

When we briefed our interior designers, we made sure the designer knew our values. Specifically, how do we divide the floor area? How much space is there for us to be collaborative? How much library space for knowledge? So values can be used in many, many ways.

How should you commission design?
To begin to answer that, let's look at different types of design. Operational design is the design of tangible things, your communications, your office, the basics.

Strategic design is much more intangible: the design of key organisational processes, strategy, the process whereby an organisation discovers its unique purpose in the world, and even how an

organisation is structured to achieve its goal
(for example, we at the Design Council have moved
from structure around administrative functions to
structure based on the customer-facing
requirements, which feels more appropriate).

Strategic design should lead the operational design.

There is a distinction between output and outcome.
It is common to frame design briefs in terms of a
pre-conceived notion of output. The secret is
trying to frame projects in terms of outcome.
Traditionally, 'I want a brochure' is a common
chant. Up and down the UK today, this chant will
ring out ritualistically. Behind this statement, what
is really meant is: 'I want new customers; I want to
operate in a new market; I am scared.'

When you look at the real issue, you may discover
what is required is a complete re-design of the
organisation. It may mean a more profound method
to achieve an outcome. To quote from the Design
Council's own guide to commissioning design:

'This section is designed to help project managers
through the design process. It'll help you
communicate your message effectively and get
the most out of the Design Council identity.
Designers should find it interesting too.'

Central planning
Design projects must be co-ordinated in the same
way as our financial planning. It is just as important
for them to fit with our Business Plan.

Action
Talk to the Design Team to put your project on to
the Design Management Schedule.

Selecting design partners and tendering
Our design partners help shape the way our
information is received by our audiences. They have
been fully briefed on our organisation's aims and
objectives.

Action
Choose a design partner who offers the skills that
you need. If you're unsure, talk to the Design Team.
If your project costs over £10,000, see the Money
Book for advice on tendering.

Before you appoint
Remember that quality of work and having the right
skills is important, but above all, you're looking for
a good partnership.

Action
Appoint the design partner who can add value to
the project. Discuss timing and costing, with the
best possible outcome in mind.

Before you brief
Be absolutely clear about what it is you want
to achieve before you brief your design partner.
If you're not sure, follow this three-point plan:
* focus on the outcome
* focus on the outcome
* focus on the outcome.

Action

Use the project proposal as the basis of your written brief.

Evaluating proposals

You're looking for an inspiring way of communicating your message to achieve maximum impact.

Action

Test the proposals with your colleagues if you're unsure about the route your project is taking.

Reviewing concepts and ideas

Remember that you're looking for inspiring ideas, and ensure that the concept displays our desired perceptions.

Action

Check that the work shows the Design Council as an authoritative, knowledgeable, innovative, effective and collaborative organisation.

Developing the concept

The concept needs to work with real pages and text, and in some cases with imagery. Make sure that in developing the idea, the work continues to display the Design Council's desired perceptions.

Action

Supply approved copy and any imagery that might be used.

Testing ideas

Everything we produce should be user focused.

Action

Talk to your audience during development to find out whether it communicates the key messages.

Notice how we emphasise/focus on the outcome.

How should you budget for design?

There is no formula for design budgets. In the big strategic design process it is less about money than time invested. There are so many variables, including the culture of your organisation. So there is not a simple answer: it depends.

To use an analogy, to what extent does your organisation give priority to design and to what degree does your organisation give priority to financial management? Do you balance the books once a year or develop monthly or weekly reports? Most organisations want some financial management. It is a priority; sometimes it is a high priority. At other times it is a maintenance issue. In this way it is comparable to design.

Everything we produce should be user focused.

Which organisations do you admire?

I really like the style of Ben & Jerry because it is a bit anti-style. If you think of Ben & Jerry with their T-shirts and beards, it's great. A key part of their style is their social contribution, which, in my view, makes them very stylish indeed. This is because I want to associate with that component of style. The Body Shop is the same. Organisations with a social drive to their activities we like. The Pepsi 'blue' campaign could have been about doing good; they would have done really well. They should have set up a laboratory doing something really meaningful like looking for a cure for cancer where all the staff wear blue lab coats. Reports on the latest discoveries could be printed on the sides of tins. Blue would have meant something meaningful instead of just different. What a waste.

Orange, the mobile phone company, has a certain style I admire. There is a consistency of approach, and clarity to its communications, which allows it to occupy a distinct, satisfactory and reassuring place in my mind. A good illustration is that when you leave a message on an Orange phone, the delightful voice of Wildfire asks you to leave a message. It is the only mobile phone company that seems to have a personality beyond the computer. It is intangible, and that is what's interesting. It gives me some confidence in the Orange brand. Someone has thought deeply about the customer experience. I want to have dinner with Wildfire, she sounds intelligent, sexy, attractive – beautiful. Isn't that cool, that I want to have dinner with Orange's computer voice woman?

The word experience is key. The experience society.

For some reason, the Salvation Army is in my mind. I am not a very religious person, but the only time I felt really good about giving money when someone tapped at my door is when the Salvation Army came down my street with their brass band. They have an earnestness and integrity that is just lovely. They have style.

Sean Blair's examples reveal a lot about the potential to be different. The appeal of the Salvation Army is its consistency and integrity in approach. This is a deliberately offbeat example, but it makes the point.

It is interesting to consider that despite the decline of a classically ordered aesthetic, the idea of history is still used as a source of pleasing and reassuring imagery. Modern pubs and bars are often full of examples of old bottles or advertisements. This is the history we understand. The global development of 'Irish theme pubs' and Café Rouge style 'French restaurants' are examples of this process in action. Ironically, memorabilia and odd idioscyncracies are now designed and mass-produced to provide a 'one-off' look for these multiple outlets. Corporations provide a form of user-friendly antiquity, patiently researched in the marketplace, to please us.

Design and designers

In 1992 Neil Svensen and I were due to present to the executive committee of a major bank. We were told after the event that the question being asked prior to our arrival was: 'Which one will be wearing a suit, and which one will have the long hair and leather jacket?'

As it turned out, we both had short hair and both wore suits, but the anecdote gives a general idea of public perceptions regarding the design industry. That it is somewhat cranky, idiosyncratic and rebellious. In the early pioneering days of the design industry this was sometimes the case. But we have grown up. Simultaneously, business is becoming less buttoned up. It is a happy convergence.

Communications consultants are generally driven by the passions of their clients. If you are working for a large company, with people you like, you become embroiled with their passions and interests.

Living corporate values

Organisations have the potential actually to 'live' their brand personality, rather than simply use the methodology as a tactic. Living by the company's core values may be anachronistic in a world where change is so frequent and profound. But even as values change, an aspect of excellence in design is a manifestation of alignment between core corporate values and the brand.

Countries are built on premises of sorts. 'Life, liberty and the pursuit of happiness' define an aspect of the American experience. 'Liberty, equality and fraternity' can partially be seen in France. But it is questionable whether these values created in bygone eras are useful or relevant for, say, an Arab worker in modern Paris, at a time when extreme right-wing political parties hold a sizeable percentage of the popular vote. The cosy aspirations of those pioneers who framed constitutions are sometimes distant from contemporary realities. In business it can be that people actually 'live' the corporate brand values to a ridiculous extent. To optimise personal performance, managers need to keep an eye on reality.

The key issue is the optimal alignment of marketing promise and operational capability. It is the degree to which you can insinuate your company into the customer's mind and then whether you can deliver on that promise.

The key is to align marketing promise with operational capability.

Hotels are one of the principal environments in which an embracing, positive experience needs to be created and style clearly creates value. The great identity consultant Michael Wolff wrote a short booklet many years ago with the idiosyncratic title *You Are a Towel*, to draw attention to the powerful role such details have in the perception of customers.

In certain industries the most important brand values are often consistency, quality, reliability and so forth. For 25 years BMW and Mercedes advertising in colour supplements has been broadly consistent. This has the effect of projecting a sense of solidity and strength. It allows the consumers to recognise and remember each communication, thereby building a large group of consistent memories inside their heads, all filed in the same place and branded with the same design.

Another example of how corporate style can leverage business benefits is through the spectacular success of Specsavers the opticians. From a modest corporate headquarters in Guernsey that provides a centralised accounting, IT and marketing function, the company has aggregated some 350 small independent opticians into a one company. Neil Svensen was approached to provide a quality look and feel across the chain. He designed for the fascia of the stores a three dimensional 'pod' which focuses prospective customers' attention.

This resulted in the new, powerful corporate identity that has emerged for Specsavers. The brand is big and therefore communicates success, value for money and quality.

This process is a very important component at the heart of contemporary capitalism. Success results in size. Size communicates success and makes a company more attractive to its audiences. Size also allows for economies of scale and increased purchasing power, enhanced communications and brand recognition. This in turn usually generates more revenues and more success. There are many exceptions, but generally this is one of the underlying forces driving globalisation.

Value statements

Bold statements can work. When Saatchi & Saatchi developed the strapline 'world class' for ICI, the campaign ended up having a very uplifting influence on the company. It prompted it to try to behave in a world-class fashion. In fact, the company at the time was strongly concentrated on the UK, but the phrase did generate energy to look further afield. Whilst the performance of ICI has not been spectacular, the huge new company Zeneca was formed out of the 'world-class' ICI. In perhaps the greatest tribute to the copywriter's skill, the phrase 'world class' has now entered general business language.

Some experts in the communications industry find it admirable and refreshing to encounter companies that have basic core values to which they have adhered consistently since their inception. Johnson & Johnson is usually cited as a good example of this admirable approach. But it should be noted that the markets in which Johnson & Johnson operate are fairly stable. It is harder to imagine core values surviving so effectively in the telecommunications industry.

It may seem dated or ridiculous now, but the old IBM commitment to providing a job for life was a true commitment. The contemporary kind of corporate values of 'innovation, innovation, innovation' are more slippery and vapid. Value statements can be useful in terms of focusing minds but they need to be realistic and measurable. You cannot say, 'We are not innovative because I have checked the innovation meter and we are at only 48 per cent.'

The implementation of these values was especially pronounced at companies such as EDS which had strong policies regarding behaviour. No beards were allowed, and a married man was expected to bring his wife and not anyone else to a corporate function.

Adherence to corporate values is becoming more strict. Many believe money now drives a harsher regime for managers. Cultures are developing that accept less dissension. This goes against the spirit of diversity.

The British Telecom (BT) brand has been well researched and thought through. But the sheer size of the company militates against achieving fast change in such a business. You can change perceptions to a degree, but holding workshops to raise awareness of design may not be enough to change the underlying company. The process of good branding is about presenting yourself differently to competitors. BT may persuade staff to care more about these issues, but brave and braver advertising may not be enough to change the public's view of the brand.

Some companies do try to match perceptions with reality. This equates to integrity, which is a commodity of huge value in the corporate arena.

Corporate style

Corporate style is about individuality and personality. All the best companies have it. Style is not neutral; it is a great motivator of people. Whatever you buy in business is just a promise, but if that promise has style to it, that style makes it powerful.

Style is the 'way' things are done. If you look at financial institutions there is very little difference in style between them. What they have unfortunately managed is to do is engineer themselves into a position where they are not offensive – but also not stylish.

In the high street there is more style than there used to be. Years ago shops would do things pretty much in their own way: their businesses were 'thrown together'. After the Second World War people simply did not have the money to be stylish. Now every shop has a defined identity. But because this has been achieved by multiple retailers, every high street looks the same, so we may have lost some of the individual style of yesteryear.

The new style emerges from market research and focus groups. This means that modern brands are incredibly powerful and well thought through, far more so than 20 or 30 years ago. However, they are not particularly exciting. Years ago, leading-edge retailers such as Heal's represented style. Style was present in exciting 'pockets', here and there. Now style is more homogenised around organisations.

Many believe that Virgin, as a company or federation of companies, has such panache and personality that it embodies the true meaning of corporate style. The fact that so many people are prepared to trust 'this man with a beard' with their money says a lot about how poor the competition was. Richard Branson offers a personal style of buccaneering adventure. People who sneer at Virgin may be pleasantly surprised when they call Virgin Direct and hear how good the sales staff are. They are completely in line with the style of the company.

Tesco is another example of an interesting company. It began as a grocer with no style at all. Today it is a fantastic business. It has been suggested its staff are far more helpful than the average business. Its buildings are pleasing. To relay a personal story, a colleague of mine was shopping at Tesco with his six-month-old child and the child was crying. Suddenly a member of staff appeared and picked up the child and walked around the store with them and helped them out to the car. It was a wonderful bit of customer service. Later on, discussing this with an employee of a major competitor to Tesco, my friend was told: 'We would sack any employee who held a child, in case they dropped them.'

This story typifies the different styles of the businesses. A Tesco employee taking a very small risk to really help a customer; the competitor, a more traditional company, thinking of problems and what might go wrong, instead of what might go right.

Kwik-Fit has a great attitude to customer relations. They offer a limited range of services in a bulk operation, but they also have an innovative approach.

Another colleague was at a Kwik-Fit depot with a nail in his tyre. There was a queue of people ahead of him, and his child began crying in the car. An employee came over and said: 'Let me rush you past the queue, I will have a word with those in front of you, I'm sure they will not mind.' In a few minutes the car was fixed and my friend was waved on, with no charge whatsoever made for this service.

Many companies seem to spend all their time screwing money out of people, but at Kwik Fit staff are empowered to make decisions about not charging. An experience like that can be exciting for a customer. In this way even a 'high-street' type company can offer personality. That is what great companies do.

An individual and flexible style allows ordinary people to do what they want to do: to serve customers. In the USA the service culture is more deeply ingrained and people are far more likely to complain when they receive poor service.

A flexible style allows people to serve customers.

Some accuse certain great British companies of failing in the customer service arena. Traditional companies, for example British Airways and Marks & Spencer, might be seen as somewhat aloof. A test of great service is to take someone difficult along – perhaps a demanding relative or toddler – and see how they deal with a difficult situation. Anyone can deal with someone average in a business suit, but how do they manage exceptions?

If a company seems impervious to customer feedback or criticism, or if there is no one to complain to when things go wrong, these are bad signs. Such companies can go a long way by looking good, but they need to keep abreast of developments.

Marks & Spencer won a loyal and devoted following by offering refunds. However, Marks & Spencer staff, some people believe, can appear slightly reserved, seldom initiating conversations. This inability to instigate much pro-active dialogue can be seen as a kind of inertia. Companies that wish to succeed in customer service need to have employees who are not aloof or inflexible. If the cabin crew on an aeroplane seem like a closed team, hiding behind their uniforms and not reaching out to people, this can present serious problems. Passengers should not be made to feel they have been let into the air crew's special club.

Communicating successfully

In terms of written communications, it is vital that companies communicate in an engaging way. Key to achieving this is the use of the active rather than the passive voice. The active involves statements such as: 'We will send you your bill.' The customer knows who is doing it, 'we', what is happening, 'will send,' and to whom it is happening, 'to you'. The passive voice, so often used in business, employs phrases such as: 'A bill will be sent.' The consumer is confused and irritated by such statements. You have no sense of who is doing what. The active is a much more engaging, correct and conversational style of writing. The passive voice is the last refuge of the bureaucrat who does not want to be blamed for anything. Consider how much stronger it is to say: 'we will do this'.

Successful brand expression requires far more than imagery or graphic design alone. A good example is the innovative proposition of a recognised expert in branding communications,

Lloyds TSB. The bank has had to embrace the new 'your life, your bank' concept far more deeply than at just the level of literature and advertising. The brand needs to be expressed in every action by staff. This presents problems however, for a large integrated organisation. Rather than trying to position the company as upper crust or streetwise, it is necessary to develop a style that can suit all audiences. Avoiding using 'he', for example, and aiming for a modern, open, conversational style. In a farsighted move Lloyds TSB has even issued guidelines on the use of the spoken and written word to staff across the bank, developed by Burton Morris, the leading consultancy in corporate linguistics.

A lot of the advice from expert consultants in this area relates to politeness and common sense. If a questionnaire needs to be filled in, then ask the customer if they would 'please spare a few minutes'. If the customer has done something as requested, it is a good idea to thank them afterwards. The style of written words can also be made to sound more like a real person speaking. Phrases such as 'I'll' and 'We'll' are more conversational and appropriate.

All these techniques serve to remind businesses that the customers are flesh-and-blood people at the other end of communications. It is about treating people with respect.

As Prime Minister, Tony Blair now talks in the vernacular, in a more direct, straightforward way. He is more often to be seen without a tie. Overall he wants to show he is more in contact with the people he serves. And that is what banks do: they serve.

By developing the right personality and style, a company can become a beautiful corporation. Corporate attitudes from a large, mainstream business need to come from the top. And they need to reflect the status and character of the business. It is the board that needs to define the purpose and strength of feeling of a company. But middle managers make it happen, and across the organisation there has to be enthusiasm, vision and commitment.

An example of this in action can be illustrated by an anecdote from Steve Morris, managing director of Burton Morris. He saw a stressed mother with three small children get on a train and pull out a form he had designed in association with Rufus Leonard. With the kids screaming in her ear, she completed the form in two minutes flat. Steve says: 'I could have jumped for joy there and then.' Corporate managers, both high and low, other employees and consultants can all make a difference and really improve peoples' lives.

There has been so much change in corporate culture over the last 20 years; many companies are barely recognisable. The old attitude of folded arms – 'It won't work here' – is passing away. Language itself has played a part in moving people from the old-fashioned ways, as it has become more open and accommo-dating. Legislative change has also come to the rescue of the consumer, with financial service law, for example, demanding that a single 'key features' document is given to customers, which must be written in plain English. Rules about the validity of contracts are also emerging which are forcing companies to be transparent and clear in their communications.

Looking ahead, it may be very difficult for big companies such as Marks & Spencer to make a comeback. The world is moving very quickly, and some of the older styles of companies have dinosaur structures that cannot respond with the necessary speed.

Style – the way companies speak – is as important as what they say. It communicates a lot of information about their integrity, commitment and attitude.

The branding proposition comes first. Your tone of voice is your way of making it happen.

The JAM approach

There are few more influential or respected views on corporate style than those of interdisciplinary design and communication group Jam. Acknowledged by major corporations, the design community and contemporary art galleries alike, Jam has burrowed into the essence of the corporate soul to develop some brilliant innovations in products and environments. Its extraordinary approach illuminates the shadowy perception of corporate style.

Style is idiosyncratic. Individuals who are stylish do not follow pre-set fashions. A corporation that plans to appeal by pasting on style is going to shoot itself in the foot. The contemporary consumer audience in London, for example, is very aware, and it will see through fakes. Style has to come from within.

If clients are attracted towards the idiosyncrasies of a particular advertising agency and attempt to adopt its style as their own, instead of looking to their own strengths, they have lost the plot. Because that superficial quality appeals to a group of clients, it develops only a superficial identity. Some clients have even boasted of how far their agencies are from the product. They feel the image is all that matters. But the really important question over the longer term is, does advertising reflect the core of the organisation?

An excellent example of how a corporation might act with style involves a product concept that has been designed with Campbell's soup in mind. An injection moulded panel has been developed with integral magnets, intended to hold soup cans and keep them readily accessible whilst showcasing their label designs, so making a feature of them. Quite gloriously the designer has dubbed the product a 'handy wall holder', in recognition of the artist who immortalised the Campbell's soup tin.

Style must emerge from the soul of a corporation. It cannot be pasted on. Ideally a company's style would be so strongly manifest throughout its operation that it would be synonymous with its identity.

Style must emerge from the soul of a corporation.

Jamie Anley, a founder of Jam, believes corporate style can be developed from a close understanding of an organisation's identity. A brand should be based on its character and not an artificial identity. Character, as in individuals, is the core strength of any organisation. Jam has worked with the major manufacturer of ladders, SGB Youngman, to produce some beautiful, strong, lightweight chairs made from their ladders. Jam saw that the company's core strength, its character, is the technology and the aluminium that it uses.

The extension of this core character into other creative solutions creates what Jamie Anley calls cultural currency. Building on this existing asset, Jam believes is preferable to utilising more conventional methods of identity creation. Although a company may have great taste, commission great advertising and produce a wonderful, glossy brochure, if there is a gap between the perception of its identity and its true character, there is more chance that its image will be misunderstood.

Character is the core strength of any organisation.

The challenge is to enable manufacturing industries to look to themselves for inspiration, to use their resources and skills to embark upon new ideas and new directions not previously considered. In this sense Jam manages external innovation programmes for its clients and thereby shows how design can be used to implement change. However big a corporate research and development department may be, there is always a benefit from having a 'visitor' come in from the outside and look at activities, with a different perspective.

One of Jam's first actions was to work with Whirlpool Europe srl, one of the world's largest manufacturers of 'white goods'. Using stainless steel washing machine drums, Jam designed furniture, stools, storage and display cabinets, and tables. Whirlpool thought this was peculiar but cautiously backed Jam's initiative.

When the designs began to win serious international recognition through magazines such as *Vogue* and in exhibitions in the Guggenheim Museum of Art in New York, Whirlpool could see that the effect of the project had been to create enormous added value in terms of media coverage for the brand. Through this collaboration, Whirlpool entered the conceptual design arena with all the positive product associations that follow. Jam's concept of communicating by design was seen to be effective and Whirlpool committed to a forward programme of work.

Overall, Jam believes that companies should welcome consultants, which it calls 'visitors', who can use their external, independent perspective, add integrity and assist in revealing the internal vision and direction of their organisations.

The conservative attitude of organisations towards investment in design can partially be explained by the current 'cost control' ethic, perceived as a 'safe bet' solution. This cautiousness inhibits innovation and results in a 'closed loop' attitude which eventually leads to vulnerability in a competitive market place. One way to overcome this attitude is to recognise design as a valid tool within the research, development and brand building function where there is already an agreed budget.

Jam acts as an ideas agency and it operates in a way that reveals something of the deep, strategic role designers can play in the direction of a company. For example, a manufacturer of very high specification durable foam, which is only used by a few companies for some specialist purposes, approached Jam to expand on the inherent potential of this material. Having gathered together a team of creatives, the project culminated in the launch of twelve consumer product designs at a show in Selfridges. The objective was to celebrate the properties of the Zotefoams material, build the brand and show it off to other designers. The exercise created millions of pounds worth of editorial coverage with numerous enquiries coming in to the manufacturer from across the world – from Disney to toy companies. The impact of this project was so great that the BBC even made a documentary about the event.

Manufacturers often underestimate their consumer audience, and fail to recognise that design is a universal language. A crucially important reason for companies to invest in communication through design is that through using design to communicate, cultural barriers and language problems are avoided. The ladder concept needs no explanation. This is a great justification for expenditure on an integrated innovations programme.

The reason why Jam's work for Whirlpool has made it into leading design galleries, and the reason it is celebrated the world over, is because of its concept, execution and the way it holds a mirror up to contemporary manufacturing industries and culture. Jam has made a plethora of products using 35 mm film because digital technology has largely replaced old photographic methods. In this way Jam operated like an artist does, responding to contemporary circumstances.

By revealing brand character Jam acts as a catalyst for focusing corporate efforts towards the future.

An example of good brand alignment is the paint launched by Benetton. This is a logical move. It is the only paint on sale world-wide with the same name used in every country. It is the first truly global paint brand. It follows naturally from the core attitude of the company, articulated consistently for over a decade: 'united colours of Benetton'.

Those companies that can liberate the potential of their staff's intelligence will prosper. Progress is inhibited when the corporation forgets that its staff are consumers. Everyone in a corporation is a consumer. But when corporations forget they are an integral part of society, the consequences are detrimental.

The idea behind generating style or cultural currency is that if you are involved in pro-active events and activities engaging people who are at the forefront of innovation – the leading fashion designers, product designers etc. – your organisation will thereby be part of the process of developing change. Your corporate involvement must be more than financial – its resources must be involved in a deeper way.

Involvement in exhibitions on design, in collaboration with credible government or other agencies, is one way to achieve recognition and achievement far in excess of what can be gained through simply buying advertising in a magazine or commercials on television. Anyone with money can buy commercials. But if you are included in editorial coverage, if you are changing perceptions, you are making the story.

The marketing budget for NASA sending a rocket to the moon is minimal. The act is so fantastic that all the world's media will trek along without any hype. If you are involved with something progressive and exciting about initiating change people will want to know about it. That is the media's role.

Generating cultural currency also has positive effects on the people within a company. The Zotefoams exercise created a whole new sense of direction inside the company. Employees who had previously seen themselves solely as a machine operator were suddenly able to see their craftsmanship on television as part of the evolving direction of design. This has given the company a real sense of mission and created a brand for Zotefoams which never existed before. A year later Zotefoams returned to Jam and asked for more.

Jam's interest in developing new product designs from a company's basic components has led to many complex benefits. The evolution of an elegant, wobble proof vase from a Philips lightbulb indicated new directions for brand promotion within the Philips Corporation. As a result of this initial collaboration, Jam was then able to learn more about the company and discovered that Philips lighting had also produced a very low energy lightbulb. This meant that it could be used safely in conjunction with vacuum formed plastic foam material. This led to a cross-collaboration between Philips and Zotefoams, adding a new dimension to Zotefoams' market potential. The collaborative design, marketed as the Saturn lamp, also allowed Philips to demonstrate the effectiveness of its low energy, low temperature technology. This is just one of a number of examples of Jam thinking its way across companies to achieve unique results. Jam also operates its own world-wide distribution organisation, which helps significantly in acquiring international media interest in the products it designs.

Corporate collaborations in the Jam communication-by-design scenario develop brand character because they use the core strengths of two companies, and use product design to communicate it. The importance of these inherent capabilities is not to be underestimated. If you draw an organisational map of a company, with concentric circles representing advertising and marketing on the outside, employees inside and the board of directors right at the centre, within this inner circle are the processes the company is based on: its key resources and its product manufacture or service. Often the outer circle has little relationship with the core, providing only a synthetic wrapping around real life in the business.

In the case of SGB Youngman, the company saw itself simply as a ladder manufacturer. But when Jam visited its factory and looked around, it saw the largest consumer of aluminium in the UK. Huge extrusions were everywhere, and the company clearly had the ability to weld expertly, as well as many other forming capabilities.

Jam suggested that SGB Youngman should change its self-perception from 'we make ladders' to 'we produce lightweight objects that support load above ground'. From this premise could come a thousand new business areas. Suddenly the company could make bunk beds for kids, garden furniture, roof racks for cars and a host of other products.

Jam is experienced enough to realise that it could not change the cultural attitudes of a company overnight. Instead its speculatively designed a range of lifestyle furniture which attracted global media coverage. SGB executives were intrigued by this response and encouraged Jam to continue. There is now SGB ladder furniture in the municipal art gallery in Manchester and it is being despatched to exhibitions across the world. It was accepted by the company that a ladder is a basic item with a limited mark-up in a competitive market. A 'ladder chair', being a lifestyle product, would not be price sensitive in the same way. In the context of product diversification, SGB is cautious to pursue Jam's line of thinking, but it is committed to exploiting the concept in terms of gaining international brand recognition.

In this way designers can and should play their part in adding value within an organisation. But to prove their value in this arena requires real commitment from the corporate client. For the first three years of business, Jam was forced to absorb the cost of pilot projects in order to build confidence with clients and to generate case studies to prove the relevance of communicating by design.

Philips, for example, is a giant global company that has design high on its agenda. But there would seem to be a paradox within the company. Undoubtedly its product designs are cutting edge, its technology is accepted as some of the best in the world and yet it seems to have failed to upstage the big name competition in terms of brand image.

Jam suggests that an example of a catastrophic disconnection between style and character can be seen in the recent re-design of a major British airline. It is easy to understand why it wished to express a multicultural identity. But the reality is that its absolute number-one brand essence was its Britishness. That is why the image strategy was reversed. Alignment with the core is the key.

Conversely, the British Airways 'Go' brand is a great success. There is a sense of oneness through the design, style and character of the whole venture, from beginning to end. It has all been thoroughly thought through.

One of the more innovative examples of corporate style in action is the former headquarters building of the Hong Kong and Shanghai Banking Corporation (HSBC) in Hong Kong. It is the most photographed building in the world. A great architectural project, which was given no budgetary or creative constraints.

Jam is creatively unconventional in its view of how a company can really excel in terms of marketing communications. Jamie Anley most admires companies that invest in themselves: for instance in their staff and their uniforms (beautifully designed and made), instead of spending the money on an extra six minutes' peak-time television advertising. Such a migration from the shriek of advertising to the more human face of business is admirable.

For Jam the practice of market research is often flawed. Jamie Anley describes the conventional methodology of consumer opinion study with the analogy of trying to deal with the lack of forward vision due to snow obscuring a car windscreen by using the rear view mirrors; using the past to deal with the future.

In some cases, companies decide to use market research to anticipate where people are going, and then try to develop a strategy around this information. This approach will inevitably lead to the expensive process of following trends.

Perhaps brand strategists should not be looking outwards at what consumers are doing, but rather looking inwards at the company's core, and generating creative concepts which will attract consumers towards their product brands. To be genuinely creative and innovative, a company needs to have the ability to change its perspective. Corporate man at the moment tends to think in a linear and sequential way. Contemporary civilisation however demands a holistic approach, assimilating many facets at the same time. Jam's role is to bridge across these approaches, to enable a comfortable shift from the purely practical to the visionary. Sometimes this is only achieved by inviting external consultants to act as a catalyst.

Perhaps the best example of this is Jam's work in uniting the DuPont subsidiary CORIAN with the kitchen appliance manufacturer Whirlpool. Jam realised that there was an opportunity to combine the expensive, quality surface material CORIAN, used in kitchens, with the technology of Whirlpool equipment.

A spectacular installation at 100% Design 1999 gave rise to several unique and fascinating consequences. Firstly, the overall aesthetic and ergonomic requirements of the ideal kitchen were recognised, simplified and improved. The potential for sales was multiplied through the combined market exposure. In addition, the imagination of Jam's associates in the project (Architects, Softroom and Lighting Consultants, Linbeck Rausch) highlighted the strengths of the respective products creating a far stronger overall effect than could have been achieved independently.

For Jamie Anley, the ideal is that, in a perfect corporation, all the employers would have such confidence and satisfaction in the organisation that they would, if you met them at a party on Saturday night, want to press a business card into your hand.

Everyone wants to be part of an organisation with vision and direction. People love to associate themselves with any project that stimulates consumer interest.

Designers need not be afraid of finance directors with their 'downsizing'. Most now realise that the designer's skill is at the heart of making money. Some 15 years ago it was something else like 'quality management' or 'just-in-time' manufacturing. Now it is design.

CHAPTER THREE

Trust is the key component in the marketing mix.

THE ROLE AND IMPACT OF CORPORATIONS

This is a fascinating and unique age. We are perhaps the only generation to experience the unlimited exploitation of natural resources by heavily industrialised technology – before the limits to growth in physical goods consumption became apparent and were part of our lives forever.

Brands help us navigate through an insane surplus of products and services. When we become sustainable, as we must – as we will – brands will give us more complex and meaningful information. Brands will become even more intelligent, powerful managers of our lives.

Selection by success

There is an emergent trend in capitalism that is important. It could be described as selection on grounds of success. Although this process applies throughout all supermarkets and shops, where the most successful and powerful brands command the premier sales positions, it can also be seen on the Internet.

Some of the most successful Internet search engines sell the results of their users' enquiries to the highest bidder. For example, if I type into a search engine the word 'bank', it might return first of all Citibank, because it will have sold this outcome to Citibank for the largest payment from any bank.

The interesting point about this endlessly self-reinforcing trend is that it suits almost everybody. Typically, a customer or prospective customer who is looking for a bank will want to find a large and successful one with ease. By paying the most to be returned first, Citibank will have partially demonstrated they are large and successful.

As globalisation and new technology put every brand in front of every consumer, selection systems like the one described above will become ever more important. It has been suggested that users of interactive television in the future may spend more money selecting content than they do on the content itself.

It is intriguing that the world's most successful payment system, Visa International, which processes over one trillion dollars annually, describes its greatest assets not as its satellite network, vast data processing centres or 21,000 member banks. To Visa, its greatest asset is its brand. Communicating the corporate brand values consistently over the years – by ensuring a certain quality and style to both the Visa organisation and their communications – has created one of the world's most valuable brands as the global authenticator.

Trust is the key component in the marketing mix. Brand managers will often tell you that the heart of branding is a promise. A sense of 'satisfaction guaranteed' nourishes and builds a brand.

There are many examples of why brands are needed to communicate this kind of guarantee. Two low-cost product brands that advertise quite heavily are Fuji and Kodak. This is because we entrust to them the most important moments of our lives. They help us store our very memories. So for the photographer on holiday, with numerous potential problems such as too much light or too little, knowing that the film is as good as can be is fundamental. It is one less thing to worry about. So we are happy to pay a premium for the best, which is likely to be the biggest. In other words, the one that can afford to advertise most heavily.

What is a modern corporation?

Companies are truly amazing organisations. As David Korten (1995) explains: 'General Motors' 1992 sales revenue roughly matches the GNP of nine countries with 550 million inhabitants, or a tenth of the world's population.' Korten fears that: 'Unlike real people . . . corporations are able to grow . . . amassing power indefinitely. Eventually that power evolves beyond the ability of any mere human to control.'

He also quotes the political embodiment of apple pie – President Abraham Lincoln – who observed just before his death:

Corporations have been enthroned… An era of corruption in high places will follow and the money power will endeavour to prolong its reign by working on the prejudices of the people…until wealth is aggregated in a few hands…and the Republic is destroyed.

Walmart Corporation of the USA has annual sales of over $150 billion, more than the GNP of Poland and Greece combined. Microsoft Corporation at the time of writing has a market capitalisation of more than $500 billion.

Contrast these figures with, for example, the UN estimation of $9 billion as the cost of providing safe drinking water for the 1.3 billion people who suffer daily horror without it.

For both commercial reasons and pride, corporations want to show how amazing they are. The tower formerly known as NatWest dominates London, just as the Chrysler building is a major landmark in Manhattan. But buildings can no longer truly communicate the epic scale of these new standard-setting authorities. Governments have court houses and town halls with which to express themselves. Corporations have to find other means.

Shell International administers annual sales ten times greater than the GNP of many countries. How can this power be expressed? One channel is through retail-outlet design. Shell has 48,000 petrol stations worldwide, which are, as far as possible, entirely visually consistent with one another. The tremendous logistical challenge involved in achieving this result is the proof of Shell's organisational capability, and a symbol of its statehood.

The increasing importance of corporate livery – and the general public's recognition of it – is part of the development of the new trend of human branding. People always want to show they are the best in one way or another. High-fashion designer labels have always been sought after. And as a sign of the attractiveness of the labels, it is becoming more common for them to be sewn on the outside of garments.

This trend is accelerating with the 'tribalising' fashion statements of youth culture, as icons such as the black leather biker jacket are superseded by the logos of highly advanced corporations such as Nike. The ubiquitous 'Swoosh' or tick logo is willingly adopted by millions of young people worldwide, and it is displayed not subtly but brazenly.

The Nike logo gives a small and probably innocent sense of identity. More disturbingly, the swastika did the same. Wally Olins, founder of Wolff Olins, and father of the corporate identity movement, described the core elements of identity given by such symbols as providing a sense of 'purpose and belonging'. We can now see new designer entrants such as Tommy Hilfiger joining the fray, attempting to brand more and more people, who would frankly rather be branded than not.

These fashion brands, including Swatch, provide a galaxy of different emotional associations and evocations that can be bought off the shelf. They are pre-prepared fashion statements to accompany pre-prepared foods.

Corporate development

Inventions have often been adopted worldwide: the spinning jenny, the steam engine or railway train are long out of patent, if they were ever in it. But recent commercial inventors have actually created and preserved lasting entities. You can trace Edison to General Electric, Ford to Ford, and Gates to Microsoft. Their special genius lies in the full corporate exploitation of the invention. Corporate development and marketing are the keys. And these are new factors in industrial development.

Administrative structures that can exploit a circumstance are more important than anything else. The system is the heart of the product. It is interesting to note that Coca-Cola Corporation of America refers to itself as the 'Coca-Cola system'. A patent is only half the story. Globalisation – global exploitation – requires the combination of corporate development, finance, logistics and marketing.

Corporations are really the standard-setting bodies in contemporary society. In most spheres they have taken over from government. Where they have a presence, they are the agents of order and prosperity. Where they are not is often neglected.

The dynamics of globalisation have resulted in a move from the historic process of 'building a business' locally across generations, to the contemporary absorption of entrepreneurial skills by larger corporate entities. With very few exceptions, those individuals who wish to create products, services and organisations with critical mass need to enter the new world market through an existing transnational organisation. In the top league, corporate success now comes in one size only: global.

Corporate success now comes in one size only: global.

The acquisition of entrepreneurial companies such as Web TV or Hotmail by Microsoft provides an example of this process. Microsoft built its early success largely as an incredibly successful parasite, which invaded the great dinosaur that was the old IBM. Using fiendishly clever licensing agreements it managed to stay independent and thrive as a great new industry emerged. Even the largest companies are responding to the trend.

Examples can be seen everywhere, from the mega-mergers of Daimler Chrysler and BP Amoco to the recent global rebranding of all businesses in the HSBC group.

Good and bad: the issues for design

The question of 'good and bad' is a complex one. Good design is good design, but are bad companies using it? And what is a bad company?

At the most fundamental level, no company is intrinsically bad. In the modern, industrialised world, the era of criminal corporations – notwithstanding the Mafia, cocaine cartels and exploitative military dictatorships – are gone.

No organisation has evil as its intent. Although this book argues that, at a systemic level, governments are fundamentally impotent and a spent force in our society, they are still capable of bringing demonstrably evil companies – like pyramid-selling companies – to account, and liquidating them.

So, are there no bad companies? The answer is depends on your perspective. If your main concern is noise near airports, bad companies will be Boeing and Airbus, British Airports Authority (BAA) and British Airways.

But what if you are most concerned about air pollution and global warming? For you the list extends to include all car companies, all oil and chemical companies, and almost all electricity companies and manufacturers. And if you are worried most about stress in the workplace and the speed of the modern world, then your list of least favourite companies will probably include almost every corporation of any scale operating exclusively within the current norms of production and marketing.

So is every company equally bad? I have great sympathy with people who campaign to limit the negative impacts of corporations in any sphere. But it can be educational when viewing a complex range of options to study the absolute extremes.

Part of the genius of George Orwell's novel *1984* is the portrait of absolute evil. By graphically describing a political state embracing absolute evil in an unceasing nightmare, Orwell shed light on the wide, complex, infinite range of political situations, and gave an absolute negative to help begin to define positive. Relevant components in Orwell's warning are the reduction in the richness of language and excessive work.

Corporations now set standards in society. Through their own operations – their bodies – they exemplify behaviour patterns that have emerged as the norms for the industrialised world. These patterns of conduct represent the aggregation of numerous estimations of appropriate behaviour by managers implementing corporate objectives with reference to a series of diverse general criteria. The standards include:

- fair (in the West at least)
- non-discriminatory
- profitable
- safe (in the West at least)
- flexible
- effective.

What is so interesting about the above list is what is missing. There is no mention of any form of meaningful aspiration, ideal, direction or much emotional humanity. This is perhaps the most damning charge that can be levelled at modern corporations. For all their size and power, despite their profound influence, they are intellectually lazy and emotionally trivial. With command of resources greater than nation states, they are financially wealthy, but spiritually bankrupt.

Corporate marketing

Corporate branding of goods and services includes:

- a methodology for signifying the extension of the corporate promise of standards into a world of products;
- a unifying emblem for co-ordinating and reinforcing marketing communications;
- a 'promise' to deliver consistently.

It is this key concept of consistency that provides the overreaching rationale behind all corporate and brand-design management. Of course there are different kinds of consistency. Every Kit Kat or Coca-Cola is identical. Blockbuster Video offers hundreds of different films, but they try to ensure they are of a consistently satisfying standard.

Many of these product promises emerged in more inconsistent times than our own. For example, Shell petroleum has traditionally advertised itself as pure, unadulterated fuel. Although petroleum is seldom watered down in Western Europe, still today the Shell brand image of product integrity has value and meaning in many countries in the world.

Corporate brand power

The BBC as an institution has a fascinating approach to design. With its remit to deliver a 'public service' this philosophy has been woven into the very fabric of the organisation. Two of London's finest surviving buildings host respectively the BBC World Service and BBC headquarters at Aldgate and Portland Place. The BBC has had, at least in the past, an ostentatious sense of its own funding security. This has led to a certain 'largess' amongst BBC employees such as would be unheard of at, for example, another great institution like Shell. However, it has produced some great work.

The corporate history of IBM revolves around collecting large amounts of money by communicating competence. Indeed, the name IBM is synonymous with corporate power and influence. Sometimes such brands are built on negative criteria. To many people IBM was famous for 'locking out' competitors. If a customer ever used a non-IBM supplier they were often 'locked-out' of their technical support system. Woe betide any company or individual who was single minded enough to try and keep their systems running without the addictive cocoon of IBM support.

The same pursuit of market dominance applies today to Microsoft, albeit against a backdrop of competition. Microsoft decides what will or will not work on 95 per cent of personal computers. And if that sounds outlandish, look at the Microsoft share valuation.

The great power of brands is to provide certainty. It was John Maynard Keynes who said that money was information about the future. So, in our day, brands aspire to offer the certainty that will help us manage in an uncertain world.

The great power of brands is to provide certainty.

There is a distasteful but highly instructive spoof T-shirt, which demonstrates powerfully what corporate branding is all about. It features the logo of Pan-Am, the now defunct airline. The white on blue globe will probably still be recognisable to most of us, but instead of the words Pan-Am, it simply has the word 'Bomb'. What the T-shirt enjoys observing is that at a time of widely felt anti-American sentiment, the bombing of a Pan-Am 747 over Lockerbie essentially led directly to the demise of Pan- Am, or Pan-American Airlines. The essential element of a brand, namely 'promise' – so important in air travel – was destroyed.

Apple computer is a brand that can be described as a victim of its own early success. Widely credited with ease of use technology superior to that of Microsoft, its main competitor, Apple broke the mould, did well, and relaxed – a fatal error in business. The first Apple graphic-user interface, designed with significant input from the mother of human computer interaction, Susan Kare, was so far superior to its competitors that Apple did not really have to 'bother'. While the ferocious marketing and licensing entity called Microsoft toured the world stitching more and more suppliers into its complex web of legal agreements and semi-exclusive self-compatible technology, Apple marketing managers were rather too busy, as one wit commented: 'arguing over the aromatherapy rota'.

The lesson here is that in industries experiencing the impact of network economies – primarily the IT industries but also all those affected by the fast growth of e-commerce – success is a brand and a brand is success. Currently consumers recognise only one size. Global. The global mega-brands attract the best engineering graduates, MBAs, entrepreneurs and suppliers. Global companies like Sony and Mercedes embody a basic truth: 'We were here yesterday and we will be there tomorrow; we are in for the duration.'

National governments are hidebound by the international mobility of corporate entities. The United Nations is a political organisation comprising the elected and unelected governments of hundreds of nations. Coca-Cola, Daimler Chrysler, Microsoft and Sony each has one chief executive. So what might take the UN a decade to debate, agree and ratify, Intel could do in an afternoon. In short, there is only one big brother that can save us from the systemic decline wrought by global corporate entities, and that is the very entities themselves.

General Motors (GM) has successfully used local branding strategies in its operations. We all perceive Vauxhall as less alien than Daewoo, but its ultimate headquarters are equally far from European shores. However, to leverage fully the immense organisational potential of the vast corporate entity behind each brand, GM has applied an endorsement to the letterhead of its subsidiaries, stating: 'Backed by the worldwide resources of General Motors'. In a business-to-business context, national ties are less important than global scale and credibility.

Category management

An extension of the basic idea of brand is the retail concept of a 'category killer'. Just as a brand provides both expectation and fulfilment of a promise, so the management of categories of merchandise can further assist consumers in organising their consumption. In preceding eras, when disparities of wealth were more pronounced, retailing would be categorised by relative wealth. At one end of the scale was Harrods, at the other, Woolworth or the Co-op. As wealth has expanded across the different strata of society in the industrialised world a new form of retail has developed, grouping product categories for all customers rather than grouping the customers themselves.

These so-called 'category-killers' such as Toys R Us and IKEA are as much about selection as product. This is an interesting case of the trends in physical media echoing those in electronic media.

Corporations sometimes develop their own unique languages. But in another sense they are actually languages in their own right. Everybody knows what a Hoover is. In discussions about categorising shopping services for interactive television systems, we have often noted that brands are categories in their own right: Tesco is food, B & Q is DIY, etc.

And what is Visa? Is it a payment system or profit-making company? The answer is yes, it is a payment system, and no, it is not a profit-making company. It is in fact a service association of 21,000 banks that have globally identified a common enemy that saps their profits, namely cash and cheques. Visa goes to war on these enemies on behalf of, and with the support of 21,000 banks. Is Visa an organisation or a medium?

Visa has no single headquaters yet it processes over $1.3 trillion each year.

Global success

The increasing level of professionalism that characterises the development of modern global corporations is symbolised by the relentless growth of the professional service firms, such as Andersen Consulting. Processes are eternally upgraded around contemporary notions of best practice, as exemplified by these consulting conglomerates which specialise in optimising organisational efficiency. This facilitates rapid global exploitation of innovation.

It is perhaps worth noting that in the realm of 'might is right' marketing, global success must be – in fact can only be – the result of the ultimate marketing muscle, the muscle of the transnational corporation.

To give an example, the popularity and global reach of Calvin Klein's CK One is largely the result of it being partially owned by, and backed by the worldwide resources of Unilever, a multi-billion dollar enterprise which boasts that it has a product in half the homes on earth.

Entrepreneurs are still igniting growth, but behind them is an organisational intensity – the implementation – that gathers strength just like water running downhill. In the global village, your neighbour's innovation today is marketed globally tomorrow.

Towards a beautiful strategy

As corporations begin to act and think globally, they also have to face global challenges – and change their strategies accordingly. One of the most serious problems currently faced by mankind is the threat of climate change. In 1998 Shell International published a brochure entitled *Climate Change*. This said:

At the very least, mankind is carrying out a risky experiment with the planet by raising the levels of greenhouse gases in the atmosphere to levels far above any seen in the last 150,000 years or more. We don't know whether this will be catastrophic...

Mankind is carrying out a risky experiment with the planet.

If Shell itself is prepared to make a statement like this regarding climate change, it seems fairly certain it is a big problem.

It should also be understood that we got into this mess with corporations and technology, and it will be corporations and technology that will be needed to get us out again. In the words of James Lovelock (1987):

We cannot solve the problem through a reactionary, back to nature campaign, because we are so integrally part of the technosphere it would be like jumping out of a liner in the middle of the ocean to swim the rest of the journey in glorious independence.

It is interesting to note that Shell is now rebranding itself through a major international advertising campaign focusing on the demands of sustainable development.

There is, however, a group of powerful companies that could massively increase both their sales and profits as a result of the planet-wide efforts to address climate change. For example, organisations that can profit through reduced CO_2 emissions include:

- renewable energy companies providing solar cells, windmills and other devices; rationale: alternative to fossil fuels;
- videoconferencing, telecommunications; rationale: alternative to travel;
- travel companies using sailing ships; rationale: alternative to unsustainable air transport;
- car hire (e.g. speed-limited, computer-monitored, unruinable cars); rationale: need to cut down on car manufacture, car hire being the logical alternative;
- home insulation companies; rationale: alternative to heating;
- local food production; rationale: alternative to food travel (statistics from the Soil Association show that food travels an average of 2000 miles to reach our dinner tables);
- art, culture and entertainment 'on-line'; rationale: 'dematerialised' products and services require small expenditure of energy to produce and transmit.

One of this book's key assertions is that for each problem faced by our species, there is a particular commercial sector that can profit by addressing the problem. The key is to establish which sectors can reasonably claim that the solution to the problem is a core business activity.

Other examples include organisations that can profit by maintaining biodiversity and reducing ecological destruction caused by industrial development:

- pharmaceutical companies; rationale: diverse natural compounds are required for developing new medicines.
- tourism, travel companies; rationale: industrialisation reduces the attractiveness of travel locations.

Organisations can also profit through combatting immense human suffering caused by exploitative industrial trade. This group includes ethical retailers: companies that choose to espouse a 'fair-trade' message, practice fair-trade policies and can thereby charge premium prices.

There are also organisations that profit by avoiding investment in unsustainable industries. So, for example, companies that offer 'ethical' investment can provide meaningful product differentiation and some immunity from the irresponsible development that inevitably results from 'financial performance only' selection criteria. Reference to criteria beyond 'top quartile' returns would effectively reduce the impossible pressure suffered by all investment managers in their efforts to beat the market.

However, to achieve this there needs to be significant changes to legislation governing the remit of authorised investment managers. This is now beginning to happen. UK legislation is being implemented to make it obligatory for all pension funds to state clearly their ethical investment policy by July 2000. Most controversially, investors have to consider avoiding investments that have unacceptable social and environmental consequences, possibly reducing their financial wealth in the process.

Sustainability product marketing

Markets influence humans greatly. But they need to be co-ordinated by a broader and more holistic decision-making process than simple purchasing formulae based on rudimentary economic models of so-called 'rationale wants'. The concepts of economic rationality and utility must be recast in a global, holistic and sustainable rationality: the only true rationality in the current crisis.

Old concepts must be recast in a global, holistic and sustainable rationality.

To address this problem I have formulated the concept of sustainability product marketing or SPM. This is explored in more detail in Chapter 5. The challenge of achieving sustainability has been brilliantly expressed by Arne Naess, the great Swedish philosopher, with his apron diagram. In essence the philosophy asserts:

- you can think whatever you like;
- you must act in a way that is sustainable (the apron drawstring, pulled tight);
- you can do this any way you like.

What educates markets? Advertising. Advertising media are currently – and traditionally – the only mass communications media for informing the buying public regarding products. Although regulated by some authorities and codes of conduct, advertisers are in no way compelled to act in the general public interest when it comes to sustainability. Moreover, they currently appear to have no incentive to act in its regard.

This is a substantial missed opportunity by advertisers. The rationale is simple: if a product or service threatens the integrity of the biosphere, and the continuance of our species, and if consumers are made aware of this threat, they will avoid the product wherever possible. Although largely untested in the capitalist system at this time, I am absolutely confident of the general appeal of this approach.

There is increasing evidence of moves in this direction from advertisers ranging from the Co-operative Bank to B&Q. To give an example, within the context of the threat of climate change, an advertising campaign could be conducted that asserted the following message:

Using a car when not necessary may well result in the death of your children in the ghastly storms and floods resulting from climate change. For your children's sake please buy a videophone. The Sony videophone system sits on top of your television and costs only £850 including ISDN installation. Let's survive. Let's use videophones wherever we can.

Such a radical campaign may seem bizarre and wrong, for which I apologise. But a similar approach has already occurred in the market and been adopted successfully by major corporations.

Dr David F. Murphy of the New Academy of Business is a leading authority on this issue and he has prepared the following summary of the experience of B&Q:

The quest for beauty is not something normally associated with do-it-yourself (DIY) home improvement retailing. When British entrepreneurs Richard Block and David Qualye opened their first B&Q DIY outlet in Southampton in 1969, the business was more concerned about the logistics of using David Quaye's Mini for home deliveries than the lofty pursuit of ideals. Thirty years later B&Q plc is the UK's leading DIY retailer with a market share of almost 20 per cent, an annual turnover of £1.9 billion and profits of £188 million. In addition to its economic prowess, B&Q is also now widely recognised as a corporate leader in the social, ethical and environmental arenas. How did the company come to recognise that 'being a good neighbour is good for business'?

In 1990 when a *Sunday Times* reporter asked the company's then marketing director Bill Whiting the following question: 'How much tropical timber do you sell and from which countries do you buy it?' Whiting told the reporter that he could not provide an accurate answer. In fact, he could not answer it at all: B&Q just didn't know!

B&Q's former chairman and chief executive Jim Hodkinson (1995) offered the following thoughts:

In PR terms, quite simply, if you don't know, you don't care. This actually wasn't really true. We did care, but we weren't doing anything about it. We said the right things, but we didn't back it up with any real commitment or intellectual understanding of the issues. There was no effective control in the way we bought timber ... What concerned me was that there was no way of preventing timber from a badly managed forest coming into my stores. When such timber did come into my stores, it was my business that was being damaged, either in the form of customer boycotts, reduced staff morale, lost sales and of course bad PR. All this undermines the pride my staff have in the business, the goodwill of our customers and the end result – lost sales.

Following some initial research on the company's tropical timber sources, and after the matter was discussed extensively in board meetings, the company decided to appoint an environmental co-ordinator. Someone who had the ability to persuade, excite and make things happen.

The new man, Dr Alan Knight, soon realised that B&Q's corporate culture would help him to get things done. Market leadership was taken to mean just that, even in social and environmental issues. Even if there were difficulties, B&Q managers knew that if it was the 'right' thing to do they should do it. Knight states that he would not have taken the job if it had been purely a PR exercise resulting in the production of glossy brochures. He was given a free rein to look at the whole product range and recommend action. The message from the top was that Knight's position had to be taken seriously.

The board provided Knight with an annual budget of £500,000 and regular, direct access to the top of the organisation.

Steps to sustainability

Famous for its Panda logo, the Worldwide Fund for Nature (WWF) is the world's largest non-governmental international conservation organisation, with more than five million international supporters, including over 200,000 in the UK. From its original focus on the conservation of flora and fauna, WWF has broadened its analysis in recent years to encompass social dimensions of environmental protection and degradation.

In 1989 WWF set the end of 1995 as a target date for the world's timber trade to be based on sustainable resources and invited business and industry to work with it towards the target. As part of this new collaborative strategy, WWF invited B&Q and other companies involved in the timber trade to attend the first WWF forest seminar for business in December 1990. 'Steps to Sustainability' aimed to educate industry about the worldwide forest crisis.

WWF's message to business was couched in terms like 'Isn't this situation dreadful?' and 'Who's prepared to go along and work with us on this agenda?' WWF's bottom-line was that preventing deforestation is no longer merely the domain of governments but is actually a company's responsibility.

Preventing deforestation is a company's responsibility.

The radical end of the environmental movement adopted other tactics in their efforts to promote sustainable forest management. These groups organised mock chain-saw massacres outside DIY and furniture stores with protesters dressed as loggers graphically depicting the destruction of the world's rainforests.

In September 1991 the B&Q board set a target that by the end of 1995 the company would only buy timber from well-managed forests. Essentially Knight had convinced the board to sign up to WWF's 1995 target.

For B&Q and the other DIY retailers, WWF was perceived as a comfortable partner. Its style and approach contrasted sharply with those of most other environmental pressure groups. WWF was the only one that appeared to be willing to consider collaboration with business and industry.

Initially, the new sustainable forests policy was perceived as an idea that was being imposed upon suppliers either by WWF or B&Q. Gradually this view changed as suppliers began to realise that the policy had the potential to provide suppliers with secured orders. B&Q sold the policy to their suppliers as a means of developing long-term relationships, enabling both to plan ahead more effectively.

B&Q buyers started to grade all their suppliers on their environmental performance, including their timber policy. A league table was published each month with each buyer's name and all supplier grades listed. Top buyers were identified. Although no bonuses were given, buyers could see how their colleagues were performing. League tables were also distributed to all directors. This introduced an element of accountability.

In January 1994 WWF and four of the DIY retailers released a Joint Accord signed by the company managing directors 'to send a clear and consistent message' to over 500 wood product suppliers in the UK and overseas. The Accord specified that 'independent certification is the key' to meeting the target. It further stated that 'independent certification bodies should be accredited by the Forest Stewardship Council'.

Alan Knight illustrates how the Joint Accord had a major impact upon one of B&Q's suppliers:

I had a supplier come to see me just after the Joint Accord was published and he said:
'That was the last straw, I was trying to resist it. I didn't believe you were serious and suddenly I saw this Joint Accord. I don't even supply the others but when I saw that I suddenly realised this is a major change in business culture'.

The basic message of the Joint Accord was that competitors were talking to each other and that they had decided to go down the same route with WWF on independent certification.

QUEST is a supplier assessment programme B&Q has been running (and developing) for six years. Altogether B&Q deals with 500 direct suppliers. In 1993 all suppliers were assessed by questionnaires, followed by eight supplier seminars and numerous supplier visits. QUEST describes how the Quality of a product includes its Ethics and Safety.

A QUEST self-assessment system has now been developed for B&Q stores. Stores are measured in areas such as compliance with legislation, waste minimisation, energy efficiency, customer and staff awareness and litter control in the local environment. Stores are graded on a five-star scale by the head office.

WWF has demonstrated that progress on complex international policy issues is possible through collaboration with business.

Profitable partnerships

There is considerable momentum for business-environmentalist partnerships. In February 1996 Unilever, one of the world's largest buyers of frozen fish, formed a partnership with WWF International to develop global standards for sustainable fisheries management. Sainsbury's and United Biscuits have subsequently joined Unilever in deciding to stop the use of fish oil from industrial fishing in European waters to conserve fish stocks. Sainsbury's and other supermarkets are also working with the Ethical Trading Initiative to implement a code of conduct on minimum labour standards for manufacturers of Sainsbury's own-brand products.

B&Q has also recognised the value of wider partnerships when dealing with working conditions in developing countries as the company's website noted in 1999:

Environmental responsibility is merging with social responsibility. Nowhere is this better demonstrated than by the growing accountability retailers and major brands now have for factories they buy from in developing nations. B&Q is convinced that we must help solve the problems. Our approach has been to tackle the issues associated with our wider trading neighbours country by country, through partnerships with development agencies across the world. Starting with the Philippines and India, in 1998 our work expanded into China.

A profitable future lies not with individual corporations but with partnerships.

CHAPTER FOUR

'Added value is by definition not objective, it's subjective. It is for that reason elusive and is fearfully difficult to quantify.' Martin Sorell

HOW
TO
GET
THERE

When Martin Sorrell built WPP into one of the world's largest marketing services groups he explained his actions at the Listener Media Lunch in November 1989 as follows:

Added value is by definition not objective, it's subjective. It is for that reason elusive and is fearfully difficult to quantify. It's a quality and qualities are often impossible to measure. But all of us know that added value exists. We know that added value is what distinguishes a brand from a mere product, what protects both volume and sales and even more importantly, margins.

We know that when everything we can quantify is equal, such as prices, or weight or availability, we choose that which we feel best about.

Successful businesses and successful brands need talent and imagination at least as much as they need capital. And client companies increasingly know it.

There is, I'm sure we'd all agree, a limit to how much costs can be reduced. But the only limit to how much value can be added is the limit of the imagination.

There is certainly a great deal of truth in this. Consistent brand expression and corporate identity are essential tools in the communications mix. Most managers understand today that to ensure every marketing communication is recognised and remembered, they all need to have a consistent label so the mind can file them away in the same place, every time. This consistent exploitation of media conveys some essence of success and power.

This chapter describes best practice in the field of design and design management through a series of practical examples and interviews with leading practitioners.

Communications programmes

Lloyds TSB is one of the top five most valuable banks in the world. In recognition of the tremendous power of the brands within the group, Lloyds TSB has embarked upon an entirely new and innovative programme designed to modify and improve the corporate tone of voice.

Intriguingly, the communications manuals issued in support of this campaign represent a natural extension of the established methodology of the design manual.

The campaign has been developed to bring a consistent quality and style to group communications. The net result is to help employees identify with customers and communicate in a more adult way.

Sometimes such communications programmes work, but at other times they do not. The vast management consultancy, Andersen Consulting, is paid a great deal of money by many of its clients just to persuade managers to stop being inhuman to each other. But of course there are reasons why those inhuman systems developed in the first place. The task for managers is to strike the right balance between the order required to manage global enterprises, with the flexibility necessary to stimulate innovation. Solutions to this dilemma are infinite. Hewlett Packard is famous for never having more than 300 people in any one building, and having no job titles on business cards. The relaxed uniforms of Dutch police officers go some way towards softening the traditional image of the police and recasts it as a service organisation.

Although religious motivations now seem anachronistic, the Quaker roots of many major companies have provided a sound ethical and business approach. As Max Weber has noted in *The Protestant Ethic and the Spirit of Capitalism*, the evolution of double entry bookkeeping coincided with emergence of a Protestant work ethic. This was an early style of commercial success, combining attitude with new ways of working.

Jack Welch of General Electric (GE) is a controversial manager certainly, but the leader of one of the world's most valuable companies. He has personally striven throughout his career to permeate GE with a culture of informality. He almost never wears a tie and wants managers to co-operate efficiently, not bureaucratically. Driven by the mantra of profit maximisation, and employing a casual style, he has driven GE to the top of the world's league of companies.

Corporate redesign at British Telecom

British Telecom (BT) has tried hard over the years to match perceptions with reality. The major corporate design programme that resulted in the launch of the now famous piper logo was delayed for many months while Project Sovereign was competed. Sovereign was designed to wake up BT employees to the fact that they were no longer a staid public utility but rather they were expected to perform.

The point being that BT did not want to signal change externally until it had been achieved internally.

That sense of alignment is a form of integrity.

Presentation strategy and tactics

One of IBM's greatest achievements, and the main reason why it was for many years one of the world's most powerful companies, is that the founder, Tom Watson, managed to reinvent entirely the concept of the sales force. By simply dressing them in smart suits he turned the image of snake-oil peddler into something more akin to the modern consultant. That development of a new attitude and style of product distribution created stupendous wealth.

It is interesting to look at the development of the Co-operative movement, and its offspring, the Labour Party. The commercial organisations comprising the movement had all suffered a similar fate, and have recently enjoyed similar advances. The sweeping victory of Labour in 1997 was accompanied by the explosive growth of the Co-operative Bank with its commercially successful proposition that people actually care about more than just money.

Marketing excellence at Lloyds TSB

A great part of the phenomenal success of Lloyds TSB Group is built on marketing excellence. In response to the question 'Does Lloyds TSB have style?', Kevin Allfrey of eMarketing explained:

Yes, I believe we do. Most people still think of banks as banking, but if you go down the route of embracing people's lives, that is a deeper relationship, a more emotional relationship. Nike and Coca-Cola sell on emotion, it is not about training shoes or fizzy drinks. Style has business benefits if it is used as a differentiator. It is used to attract people, to stand out.

Companies with style in financial services include First Direct. Such companies have packaged themselves stylishly. Style is part of the brand. It is much more than the corporate colour or imagery used, it is the experience. An unstylish person in an Armani suit is still unstylish. A useless organisation with a nice logo is still useless. It is all about the total experience.

A useless organisation with a nice logo is still useless.

We have a new brand as a result of the merger between Lloyds Bank and TSB. Part of the exercise has focused on making the bank look more contemporary with a new logo, a different typeface and refreshed corporate colours, but it is also a more substantial exercise. The brand is also about the way we interact with our customers. This is a bigger issue than just communicating in plain English; rather it is about treating our customers as individuals and hitting the right tone. People throughout the organisation are being actively trained to embrace these ideas and we are finding that it makes a great difference.

Looking at the impact of brand values, it is interesting to see very senior people and people outside of the Marketing department actually espousing the brand values. We are looking to build a long-term relationship that will give us the opportunity to sell our customers many products over many years. The relationship will be of benefit to both our customer and to Lloyds TSB. A brand is not just a colour, a logo, a typeface. It is about an approach, a style. Those things that we believe begin to give that brand personality.

To give an example of an approach, the First Direct brand is upbeat, aggressive, youth-orientated. But we recognise that not all our customers will want to be treated like that. What is required is relevance. Your needs change, so the organisation you bank with needs to change as well, to match your needs. It is not just about relations with customers but rather the entire organisation.

British Airways has talked about this key aspect of marketing. Even if all the other parts of the marketing mix are in place, even if the aeroplanes look superb, the signs look great and the advertising is fantastic, if the first person a customer speaks to is rude, then it is all ruined. The world's favourite airline with the world's rudest staff would never work. Successful brands work in a different way. Lloyds TSB will build a relationship of trust with you. British Airways do the same. You trust it and it becomes your favourite. For other brands it is about a product rather than a relationship. Nike is about fashion. People become attached to brands of cigarettes and beer. They are prepared to pay twice as much for them.

The brands have different strategies. Holsten Pils is creating an image for itself that can be leveraged over the long term. It uses positioning of quality to gain longevity in marketing. Stella Artois has a similar approach with its draft beer and cans, but interestingly, Stella produces more adventurous bottled beers like Stella Dry, to catch the more fashionable end of the drinking market. The very successful bottled beer Sol was definitely 'cool' at the time of its launch because it was new and different, with the novel inclusion of a fresh slice of lime at the bar.

Branding on the Internet

Building on the lessons of the conventional media, on the Internet marketing is therefore about much more than look and feel. I think it is easy to talk about achieving the whole brand experience on the Internet, we can all see the possibilities. But creating the business case to do it all properly is difficult. The Internet is unique because it can lead you through a whole experience of the product. A banner advertisement can lead you right through to accessing your bank account.

On the Web, users can interact with the brand, and the technology permits personalisation. However, there are also significant drawbacks. For example, when we send a printed item to a customer, we control exactly how it looks and feels, the texture and colours etc. On the Internet we do not have so much control. Odd typefaces may present our words. Our corporate colours may be distorted and we cannot control that.

For this reason, we must learn to leverage the brand on the Internet in different ways, by focusing on such matters as tone of voice, interactivity; generally those things that the user has not got an opportunity to change.

Auditing your positioning

The approach to take depends on who you are. A massive operation like us will take advice from leading external agencies such as Rufus Leonard and Wolff Olins. A one-man band can think this through for themselves. It goes back to standard textbook stuff:

- What is our mission?
- What are our objectives?
- Who are these people and what are they trying to achieve?
- Are they characterised as traditional, young, energetic?
- Describe your audience.

The approach is down to different individuals and is open to debate. Experimentation is key. You have to make a statement, try it, and maybe change it. Find out what fits, find out what works. These are key points. These things should not be set in stone. The world changes and the Internet changes faster.

Looking ahead, I think Internet materials will re-invent themselves. An Internet year is like five years. For Lloyds TSB as a whole we need to become more dynamic. I think the brand will grow with us. We have developed a brand that is capable of growing *because of the people we are working with. Launching the combined brand for Lloyds TSB is not a job over, but a job begun. That is the key difference in a proper approach to branding.*

The brand is a living, breathing thing. You have to nurture it, feed it, and water it, so it grows with you. You do this by constantly reviewing the brand, revisiting your assumptions, where you come from. It involves looking back at the organisational goals, the competition, and the political climate. Strategy doesn't just mean growing by 10 per cent each year; it is about never thinking it is over. The objective is to keep cycles of product development going, getting feedback, learning more, doing more. The day you stop listening to the markets, to customers, is the day you die.

The day you stop listening to the markets is the day you die.

The Johnson & Johnson Credo

Johnson & Johnson is a highly successful global manufacturer of healthcare and consumer goods, with a turnover of some $50 billion.

General Robert Wood Johnson, who guided Johnson & Johnson from a small, family-owned business to a worldwide enterprise, had a very perceptive view of a corporation's responsibilities beyond the manufacturing and marketing of products. As early as 1935, in his pamphlet *Try Reality*, he urged his fellow industrialists to embrace what he termed 'a new industrial philosophy'. Johnson defined this as the corporation's responsibility to customers, employees, the community and stockholders.

But it was not until eight years later, in 1943, that Johnson wrote and first published the Johnson & Johnson Credo, a one-page document outlining these responsibilities in greater detail. Johnson saw to it that the Credo was embraced by his company, and he urged his management to apply it as part of their everyday business philosophy.

The Credo, seen by business leaders and the media as farsighted, received wide public attention and acclaim. Putting customers first and stockholders last was a refreshing approach to the management of a business. But it should be noted that Johnson was a practical-minded businessman. He believed that by putting the customer first the business would be well served – and it was.

The corporation has drawn heavily on the Credo for guidance through the years. At no time was this more evident than during the TYLENOL® crises of 1982 and 1986, when the company's product was adulterated with cyanide and used as a murder weapon. With Johnson & Johnson's good name and reputation at stake, company managers and employees made countless decisions that were inspired by the philosophy embodied in the Credo. The company's reputation was preserved and the TYLENOL® acetaminophen business was regained.

Today the Credo lives on in Johnson & Johnson stronger than ever. Company employees now participate in a periodic survey to evaluate just how well the company performs its Credo responsibilities. These assessments are then fed back to the senior management. Where there are short-comings, corrective action is promptly taken.

Over the years, some of the language of the Credo has been updated and new areas recognising the environment and the balance between work and family have been added. But the spirit of the document remains the same today as when it was first written.

When Robert Wood Johnson first introduced the Credo within Johnson & Johnson he never suggested that it guaranteed perfection. But its principles have become a constant goal, as well as a source of inspiration, for all who are part of the Johnson & Johnson family of companies. Over 50 years since was first introduced, the Credo continues to guide the destiny of the world's largest and most diversified health care company.

Johnson & Johnson: Our Credo

We believe our first responsibility is to the doctors, nurses and patients, to mothers and fathers and all others who use our products and services. In meeting their needs everything we do must be of high quality. We must constantly strive to reduce our costs in order to maintain reasonable prices. Customers' orders must be serviced promptly and accurately. Our suppliers and distributors must have an opportunity to make a fair profit.

We are responsible to our employees, to the men and women who work with us throughout the world. Everyone must be considered as an individual. We must respect their dignity and recognise their merit.

They must have a sense of security in their jobs. Compensation must be fair and adequate, and working conditions clean, orderly and safe. We must be mindful of ways to help employees fulfil their family responsibilities.

Employees must feel free to make suggestions and complaints. There must be equal opportunity for employment, development and advancement for those qualified. We must provide competent management, and their actions must be just and ethical.

We are responsible to the communities in which we live and work and to the world community as well. We must be good citizens – support good works and charities and bear our fair share of taxes. We must encourage civic improvements and better health and education. We must maintain in good order the property we are privileged to use, protecting the environment and natural resources.

Our final responsibility is to our stockholders. Business must make a sound profit. We must experiment with new ideas. Research must be carried on, innovative programs developed and mistakes paid for. New equipment must be purchased and new facilities provided and new products launched. Reserves must be created to provide for adverse times. When we operate according to these principles, the stockholders should realise a fair return.

Getting it wrong

Multiple layers of management, large corporate headquarters, unimaginative internal communications, an authoritarian tone of voice, dull presentation – all these conspire to create a 'them and us' culture, which is likely to foster chronic inefficiency and waste.

A 'them and us' culture fosters chronic inefficiency and waste.

There are many examples of this kind of inappropriateness. Gerald Ratner's extraordinarily inappropriate comments illustrate how the wrong tone of voice can almost instantly liquidate a company. After the media furore created when Gerald Ratner said his products were 'crap', the Ratner name had to be buried. Lord Hanson's preference for acquiring and then breaking up companies that had poorly produced annual reports shows how competence – or lack of it – can be conveyed by the quality of design in communications.

Even ergonomics can help achieve corporate purpose – as demonstrated when it goes wrong: just look at the appalling office design of the 1970s and 1980s. Great ugly tower blocks litter the periphery of our cities. Usually derelict, these monstrosities have often contrived in their owners' demise. The near collapse of Lloyd's of London shows how environmental liabilities are now a mainstream business issue. Dr Julian Salt of the Loss Prevention Council, an advisory body to the insurance industry, has commented how the spectre of climate change is now so serious that insurance companies should stop investing in carbon intensive industries, making 'a rod for their own backs'.

Shell is a company with a very distinctive style. It could be described as arrogance or confidence, depending on your perspective. Shell people will tell you that if the company was a school, it would be Eton. If it was a shop, it would be Harrods. The company's reputation of strength and competence can be seen in the famous corporate strapline – 'You can be sure of Shell' – a sentiment that used to be echoed by many happy investors.

Recently, Shell's financial performance has not been so impressive. The former Shell chairman Cor Herstroiker commented on the review of the group following the Brent Spar and Nigeria incidents: 'We looked in the mirror and did not like what we saw.' This is a major issue following the launch of the multi-billion dollar Retail Visual Identity programme which, in the words of former marketing co-ordinator and now group managing director, Steve Miller is intended to: 'fully exploit the strength of the Shell brand'. What use is that money if the Shell brand is soiled?

Getting it right

Sony and Harrods are two companies that have successfully managed to encourage in every employee a pride in quality communications. The legend that is Rolls-Royce motors shows us how positioning alone in a market can translate into style. Modern corporate identities such as Orange and First Direct show how graphic design can be a powerful weapon in creating meaningful distinction in the minds of consumers.

Constructing the right office environment has been a significant component in the extraordinary success of Loot, the global listing service, and one of Britain's most valuable private companies.

British Airways' innovative new headquarters is a place where managers and employees are compelled to walk past each other as they leave the car park. The new offices also have as the central feature a mocked-up jetliner which is used for training – a permanent reminder to staff of the core business.

The power of a positive attitude – conveyed in the appropriate tone of voice – can be seen in companies such as Lloyds TSB, The Body Shop and Virgin. Despite being a billion-dollar company, Virgin has an 'anti-establishment' element at the heart of its brand values. The Body Shop is widely regarded as a business with a heart, because of its many ethical campaigns. Its strident tone of voice is seen by many consumers as very empowering and original.

The firm control that Boots the Chemist has over its high-quality retail environments is another an example of how success can be built on an all-embracing style that communicates trust and competence.

Xerox Europe recycles 93 per cent of its old copiers and turn them into new copiers. It has stated its corporate objective as 'zero' landfill, meaning zero per cent of its rubbish will simply be dug into the ground. It uses its environmental credentials very successfully in marketing, and its recycling systems are deliberately designed to echo nature. In this way, its recycling appeals to – and locks it closer to – its customers.

Corporate identities

James Dyson, the brilliant British designer and inventor of the bag-free vacuum cleaner, has stated that his mission is to introduce such a radical change and improvement in the supply of home cleaners that Dyson will replace Hoover as the verb used in everyday language to describe floor cleaning. But how did corporate names such as Hoover and Walkman ever become generic names in the first place?

A growing majority of the population in the industrialised world are 'cash rich and time poor'. Although clearly we all have exactly the same amount of time, what this phrase refers to is that fast diminishing luxury known as 'free time'. And accompanying our submersion in ever larger oceans of work has come astounding prosperity, if not increased equality. So for many millions of people, the aim when shopping or selecting services in their limited 'free time' is to do it rapidly. However, the same astounding wealth has confused the issue by providing ever-wider ranges of products. So product brands and corporate identities are vital elements in selection and reassurance.

In fact, this has always been the case. The precursor to modern corporate design was the heraldry of kings and queens. Coats of arms symbolised and defined groupings of political power. Prague Castle is festooned with heraldic imagery to demonstrate the loyalty and support of disparate powers across a turbulent region.

In more recent history, the best doctors would be certified and would display their accreditation in order to increase custom. Masonic symbolism was developed to provide an assurance of quality. These trends gave rise to the profession of accreditation agents.

Established traditions of corporate symbolism allow us to make split-second decisions when we are faced with huge amounts of information. For example, I might be called upon to read the following paragraph:

This product was researched, developed, designed, manufactured and marketed by a significant global corporation with an established reputation for innovation stretching back over 20 years. The company has a huge globally installed base of devices ranging from televisions to videocameras and including PCs, Hi Fi and personal stereos. All these are produced to a reliably high standard, are easy to use and come with simple, clear instructions.

Or I could see the familiar logo saying: 'Sony'. The latter is certainly more succinct than the former. They both say the same, only one is quicker.

Over millions of years, thoughts have been codified into language through words. In a far more accelerated process, categories of products – and the companies behind them – are evolving through the symbolic language of brands.

Categories of products evolve through the symbolic language of brands.

Sometimes branding and packaging performs a very simple role. It allows people to know what something is. For example, those of us who shop in a hurry, and have fairly poor eyesight, may dislike shopping for shampoo. In the chemist or supermarket one is overwhelmed by a massive selection that is almost impossible to comprehend. It may even be extremely difficult to decide which bottles are shampoo – in frustration you may well grab the nearest bottle of shaving foam thinking it is shampoo, and take it home in error.

Brands such as Timotei shampoo combine television advertising with a distinctive bottle design. The public associate the bottle with shampoo. This helps selection in shops and boosts sales.

One of the most compelling ways to get a brand under the consumer's skin is to get them to refer to the brand or its advertising in every-day conversation. A good example would be the millions of people who still say: 'It refreshes the parts other beers cannot reach.' Whatever the context, they will in some way be thinking of Heineken.

The large UK advertising campaign from Cadbury under the banner 'Thank Crunchy it's Friday' was perhaps intended to have the same effect. Interestingly this phrase has received a lot of attention. There is a chain of restaurants called TGI Fridays, in reference to the irreligious phrase 'Thank God it's Friday'. Chris Evans has a television programme inexplicably titled TFI Friday. These different references to the phrase raise its profile. It is the same process that occurs as the different promotional activities for each football team together increase the general interest in football 'the game'.

It is the genius of a marketeer to create a personal relationship between the consumer and a name. Good examples include the Apple Macintosh computer, known universally as a 'Mac', the Coca-Cola abbreviation of 'Coke' and Sony's brilliant development of the generic title of Walkman.

Brand associations

The world's leading companies express a range of brand values. Examples include:

- Sony – quality, ease of use
- Mercedes – engineering excellence
- Coca-Cola – fun, cold, refreshing
- Marlboro – cowboy style
- McDonald's – ubiquity, children friendly.

These attributes are well understood and even enjoyed by many people. An RAC car repair-man once commented on the motor of my old Mercedes: 'They are just so brilliantly designed.'

Brands and their design can serve to reassure. A brief study of the shelves of a German supermarket will reveal the preference for a subdued, 'homely', reassuring Germanic typographic style and palette.

A brand is ultimately the proclamation that a product is better than the competitors. That is the brand value encapsulated in all brands.

The design of logos

The design guru Wally Olins believes that corporate identity is about actually making business strategy visible through design. This analysis would seem to overstate the power of the non-verbal language of symbols. But it is certainly true that the character of abstract artistic expression – in the form of corporate graphic design – can communicate something of the character of corporations.

Ten years ago I had a series of discussions on the design of logos with the managing director of Rufus Leonard, Neil Svensen (the designer of this book). The contention was this: does it matter if your logo is a nasty drawing of dead goat's head? After much debate Neil convinced me that it did not matter what the logo of a company is, so long as it is implemented consistently and to high quality in all media. The logo or identity is in this analysis like a telephone number. It does not really matter what it is, but how you answer the telephone is what's important.

Sean Blair of the Design Council feels this attitude is rather crude and cites the identity of the clothing company Mambo which is: 'all over the place', but it works. He feels perhaps the challenge is perhaps for corporate identity to be 'an honest, healthy reflection of the culture, system, processes, vision and values that it claims to support'.

In design the challenge is to avoid looking fragmented, confused and disorganised – just a group of small-scale, amateurish companies sharing a name and perhaps some variants on a corporate colour. Instead the aim is to look consistent, competent and focused. Achieving absolute consistency in the implementation of a corporate design style demonstrates that the corporation is disciplined and organised and pays real attention to detail.

The aim is to look consistent, competent and focused.

Consistency in design of this kind usually saves money because it means inventing the wheel just once. Most importantly, by using the corporate identity in the same place, in the same style, in the same colours, wherever it appears, helps the public to recognise and remember every time they see the logo. It allows consumers to file away in their brains these messages in the same place, so they build up a full understanding of the size and scope of an organisation.

This work is entirely separate from the design of logos. Often design companies will win a corporate identity project by gathering examples of all the different versions of the theoretically single logo together, presenting them on a number of boards showing all the different types of compliment slips etc., and then the client can usually understand immediately that something must be done. In addition the cost savings that result from standardisation, central purchasing and the avoidance of duplication are significant.

To give an example, as part of the corporate identity project for Kleinwort Benson Investment Management, Rufus Leonard reduced 52 different types of printed envelopes to seven basic varieties. This resulted in considerable cost savings. This again has nothing to do with design or redesign of a logo – a task that needs to be undertaken every 10 or 20 years. It is rather a matter of design management, which is a process that needs to be undertaken every day. It is in fact a great truth that the more resources and energy a company devotes to managing design every day, the less frequently is will need to suffer the hideously expensive and disruptive task of redesigning its logo.

It is worth noting that the logos and symbols for four very strong brands – Orange, Shell, Blue Circle and Eagle Star – have one of the greatest possible strengths of any identity design: namely, the logo is a visual representation of the name. Unsurprisingly, in consumer research, such companies tend to have the highest recognition records of company name, from the logo alone.

Creating a new business at ONdigital

ONdigital is widely respected as a leading provider of digital television services in the UK. Its marketing strategy has been a hugely successful. Marc Sands, director of brand marketing, spent eight years working in advertising and one year as marketing director of Granada UK Broadcasting before taking the hot seat at ONdigital. Marc Sands says he was electrified at the prospect of helping to establish a new business from scratch.

As one of the first employees, Marc Sands was involved with every aspect of defining the culture of the company. This included choosing the name, how the offices should look and defining the whole attitude and style of the company. It was a completely clean state. With around £100 million in the marketing budget, Marc Sands describes it as dream stuff.

One of the key drivers behind the birth of ONdigital was the desire to migrate television away from the analogue signal ranges. This is so the government can sell them, but also so that consumers can enjoy more of the potential of digital media.

Digital television has the potential, like the PC before it, to significantly affect people's lives. Granada and Carlton – two major companies with interests in independent television – combined to pitch for the licence for digital terrestrial and the government decided they were the most suitable for the task. With financial muscle and significant media assets, ONdigital was chosen to pioneer this unprecedented new technology, which was previously untested anywhere in the world.

Marc believes – and the success of ONdigital seems to prove – that the offer from Cable and Sky of 200 channels is somewhat meaningless. He observes, correctly, that short-term to mid-term, say over the next ten years, there will probably be a core of popular channels, with niche programming growing only slowly at the periphery.

ONdigital has seized this opportunity and is beginning to establish itself at the core of national television consumption. In essence, Marc Sands believes that popular television cannot be made for the small sums expended on niche activities. This perspective reinforces

the call made in the mid 1990s by David Mercer, head of design at BT, for quality television production to cost less.

Marc describes style as a way of doing things. Both the service itself and the more peripheral aspects. Style is expressed through your entire front end – from your advertising to your offices and point of sale. All these elements, although a superficial skin, need to reflect the underlying business. This is the key to delivering the promise of a brand. If you over-promise, if you over-stretch, the gap between delivering the promise and service is too wide. Matching the two is the key.

The successful style of ONdigital is very open. There are no offices, everyone has the same size desk, and there is nowhere for anyone to hide. That says something about them – open, trusting and unconcerned about people looking in on them. They have confidence. There is no hiding. ONdigital aims to make things as simple as possible, and it aims to avoid the corporate bullshit. The battle is not won, but it is trying.

Marc Sands says that when he got buy-in from the senior people to have an entirely open-plan office environment it was a great achievement. ONdigital plans to be a very straightforward organisation. He was heavily influenced by working at the innovative advertising agency Howell Henry Chaldecott Lury, which made him see new ways of working.

The combination of 'hot-desking', home-working, offering Internet access to employees and generally reducing formality persuaded Marc Sands there was another, better way of doing things. He believes creativity is seldom achieved in a closed environment. At ONdigital there is a very horizontal organisational structure. Job titles are an anachronistic requirement to which people pay scant attention. Basically, if you want to do something, the attitude is get on and do it.

Marc Sands believes the style of ONdigital can free itself from the peculiar history of the industry. Perhaps Bill Gates entering the UK industry will change this but basically pay-television has not won public confidence. Their entire business plan is based on trying to charge you for what you enjoy.

ONdigital realised that in this fragmented, low-trust industry there was scope to behave in a proper and decent manner. It is trying to occupy that space.

Marc Sands is an expert in selling new technology and his recipe is simple:

Nobody is interested in technology. Don't talk about it – people don't understand it and are not interested in it. The way to sell it is on the benefits. Focus on that. If you take the word interactivity, that is a great word. But it is impossible to understand. When Sky launched they focused on interactivity and On Digital were so happy. Because people don't know, care or understand, or are in anyway interested in the abstract concept of interactivity.

The truth is that they will be soon, because interactivity is brilliant. But if I talk to you about a single subject, and you don't know about it, we are not going to have a conversation. You have to deal with people in small steps. It may seem patronising, but it was the same for me. I didn't understand it when I first saw it. Television is a passive medium. If you suddenly say to people: 'Shop, bank, do it all over the television,' that is a shocking idea, people get switched off by it. People want to say: 'Wooah, slow down.'

Research shows people have traditionally wanted more and more channels. Requests for interactivity were bottom. They are slowly rising, but it will take some time. Interactivity will be phenomenal but it will take time to evolve. Even now, the real experts do not know what will happen.

The attitude at ONdigital is to get on with it. In the words of Marc Sands:

We are running so fast, we don't have any mission statement. We all know what we are doing. We are here for a reason. We need to get X subscribers by Y date, but that does not mean by any means possible.

The attitude at ONdigital is to get on with it.

We don't have a mission statement that can last for more than one day. For us, at this stage of development, that makes sense. There are very few airs and graces. It is too rollercoaster a business to set your views in concrete.

As you move further and further from head office you get back to basics. We have four call centres. We tell them about our culture. Like why we are called 'ON'. We are simple and straightforward. There was an idea to call ourselves 'Mint'. But it was realised that the business was, must be, more simple and straightforward. It all goes back to that idea of being simple and straight. We argue all the time, but that is okay, because we all know what we are trying to do.

Successful marketing

Marc Sands believes the two defining characteristics of developing successful marketing communications are:

- don't lie
- if you are smart, and believe you are right, you probably are.

Other companies Marc Sands admires include Nike. Nike gives 90 per cent of a dream but leaves 10 per cent for you. Nike has got the basic product right, which is the starting point. But it has also completely understood the way the consumer responds to personality, sports gear, and that whole way of life. It has defined it. But it has only defined it so far. Nike provides the sporting heroes, but when you put the running shoes on, it's you. It has taken you right there but given you room to be you. It doesn't tell you the whole story; it leaves room for you to play a part in it. Nike has had moments where it has defined a way of being that is incredibly aspirational and in your own way, achievable.

Marc Sands believes brands in new media will have to follow the same procedure as brands in old media. The same textbook lessons apply:

- be the first
- offer people something they want
- deliver what they want.

The Hoover building is an art deco masterpiece now owned by Tesco

That does not mean the old school brands will necessarily succeed in the new world, because they are hidebound by success in the old. The older companies have experienced a development curve: they began as entrepreneurial, taken risks, then changed, and become defensive. Unless they can keep taking risks, they will die.

Successful branding means just one thing: don't lie. Know yourself and your organisation. Companies have to say what people want to hear. They have to run as fast as people.

More than ever, consumers are fickle: they leave you, they migrate. There is, however, more and more feedback coming in from customers – from call centres, from e-mail – and that is a great resource to exploit. It is the democratisation of commerce. The lead-time of product development is shrinking because of competition. People now have more and more choice, and people are taking advantage of it.

You can now start an Internet-based company in a year and be a billionaire. Marc Sands is very conscious of the scale of what he is doing:

We have the capacity, indeed the potential, to influence hundreds of thousands, perhaps millions of people's lives. I personally feel an element of ethical and social responsibility. I aim to behave in a way that hopefully the majority will find acceptable. Business is inseparable from the outside world.

Marc Sands summarised his comments by asserting his belief that digital media will grow massively and could democratise hugely. It will either implode on itself because it has no order (and people love order), or it will change people's lives for the better. Because it is really up to you if you get involved in a way that has never been possible.

Corporate retail identities

Generally, retail designs evoke attractive emotions such as strong, modern or wild. This visual language is always building on itself and always evolving. The goods are displayed beautifully, in beautiful lighting, showing off their beautiful colours. A good cosmetics shop is a feast for the eyes and senses.

At the more rarefied and expensive end of the market, it is often the case that a modern clothes shop is a gallery of brilliant, bold interior design, and even architecture. The top of the market defines itself through beauty.

Swatch

The creation of the brilliant 'Swatch' brand was a response to the national economic catastrophe in the 1970s, when Japanese computerised watches threatened to liquidate the Swiss watch business. With an eye to the deeper essences of branding and loyalty, the small, stylish country of Switzerland included their flag in the Swatch (Swiss-watch) logo. Through excellence but not conservatism in design management Swatch has put Swiss watches back on the map. The Swiss are inventive at building on national associations in product marketing. Near Leicester Square in London is the huge complex of the 'Swiss Centre', as well as a large sign showing the Swiss flag and the cantons of Switzerland. At many levels, that investment helps all Swiss businesses, although it is practically impossible to quantify.

Häagen-Dazs

This tremendously successful company has virtually rewritten the rule book in terms of developing and launching a brand. The look and feel of the shops evoke some of the details of quaint old ice cream shops, but these have been aggregated into a simple retail design.

The launch of Häagen-Dazs in the UK combined brilliant PR with unprecedented advertising. The PR campaign involved giving Häagen-Dazs away free at 'society' events like horse races and exclusive social venues. This created coverage in the glossy magazines which was then amplified through innovative mass marketing. Highly erotic imagery, combined with brilliant PR made frozen dairy products both high class and sexy. No ice cream company had ever tried this kind of approach before. The product was and is very good, but the marketing and branding was exceptional.

Brand management at Shell

The vast multinational formally known as the Royal Dutch 'Shell' group of companies has referred to itself as the world's largest retailer, with 48,000 retail outlets worldwide. An employee of Colorlux, the leading European sign manufacturer, has suggested that Shell, like McDonald's, simply own the 'best' colours. Burger King has a similar palette, and this implies there may be some common emotions created by red and yellow that are particularly appropriate for convenience purchasing.

Shell takes its brand extremely seriously.

DELIGHTING THE SENSES & PLEASING THE MIND

Shell is committed to contributing to sustainable development – for good business and social reasons – and to cutting emissions. The Kyoto mechanisms embody the principles of sustainable development and we embrace them. All of us want to tackle this problem. Business, if encouraged properly, can provide the underlying drive for the campaign to decrease emissions. We are working with our customers to reduce their emissions.

Let business experiment – and let the customers decide. We are investing half a billion dollars over five years in solar cells, biomass and wind power. Mobilising the immense resources and ingenuity of business is, we believe, the best way of combating emissions. It may be, in reality, the only way. We believe that, if the policies are right, business can make a truly earth changing contribution.

Business can deliver creative solutions to these seemingly intractable problems. Shell has made a clear commitment to Kyoto and we will deliver on it.

Mark Moody-Stuart; Chairman of the Committee of Managing Directors of the Royal Dutch/Shell Group 08 October 1999

Listening and
Responding

Mercedes-Benz

jam

Jam's off the wall approach to design and business, since they began in 1994, has brought them to the fore front of experimental and cultural design activity.

They are best known for injecting creativity into the heart of manufacturing organisations, enabling these large corporations to perceive their existing resources in a new way, bringing companies core resources into the limelight of contemporary culture. This Jam project implementation is now acknowledged as generating brand character, an integral and visionary communication strategy which helps to project brand leaders into the future.

Jam's excitement lies in the diversity of results from any given brief - the last four years have seen Jam deliver innovative product design, fashion accessories, furniture installations, sculpture, exhibitions, lighting design and interiors.

Jam firmly believe in their responsibility as a design led communications company that their role is conceptualising futures and envisioning change.

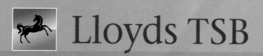

Lloyds TSB

On 28 June 1999 the national roll-out of the single Lloyds TSB brand was completed following the enactment of the Lloyds TSB Act 1998. This has brought together some 2,400 former Lloyds and TSB branches under the Lloyds TSB name and has laid the foundations for increased cost effectiveness from a simplified branch network and the move towards a single IT platform, and material service enhancements for customers.

The group has also developed a number of alternative distribution channels in order to offer the broadest possible range of access points for customers. PhoneBank, the telephone banking operation, is now one of the largest in Europe with 1.3 million customers. A personal customer Internet Banking Service was successfully launched in November 1998 and in March 1999 an Internet Banking Service was launched for business customers.

Sainsbury's

We aim to deliver an imaginative programme of community involvement that reflects our strengths as a business and meets the expectations of our customers and staff.

Each year   hundreds of charities are helped and priority given to those projects which offer some form of Sainsbury's store involvement. In this way, we help generate a high awareness of the projects within the community.

Sainsbury's Arts Sponsorship Programme was established in 1981 and has won many awards for excellence over the past 18 years. We aim to deliver high quality, imaginative and dynamic arts sponsorships, which involve as many people as possible in the communities where we trade. We create our own unique Sainsbury's schemes as well as lend support to particular regional and local projects.

The Keepsake by Kate Bunce (1898-1901)
Birmingham Museums & Art Gallery.

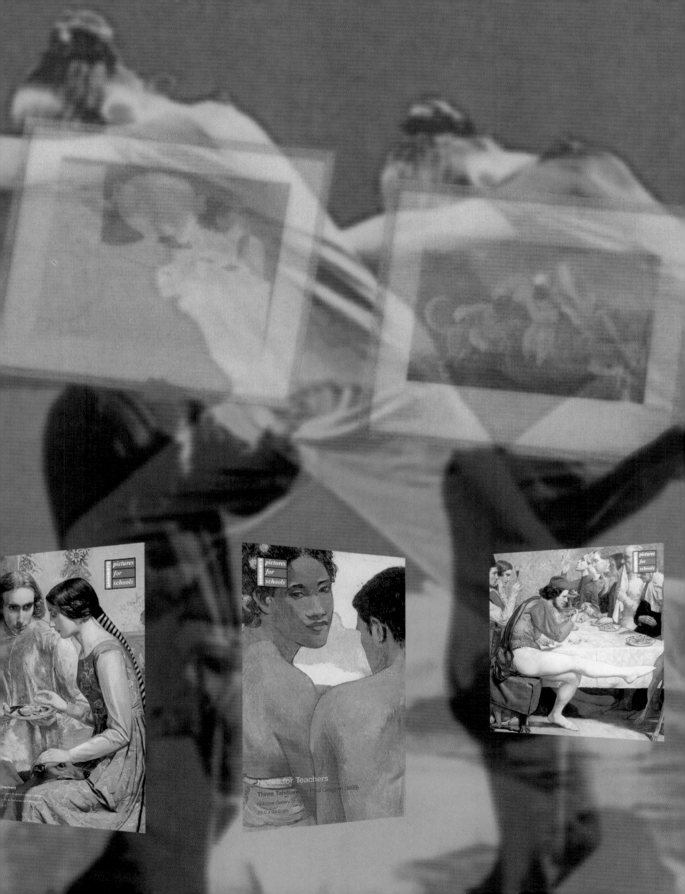

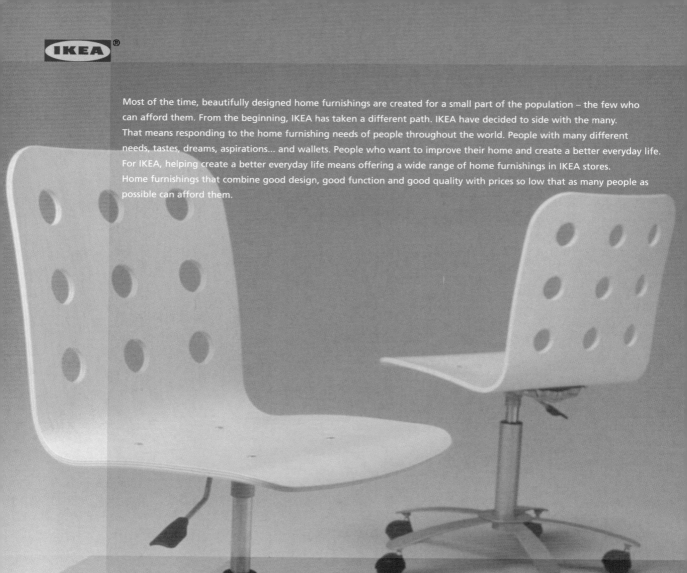

Most of the time, beautifully designed home furnishings are created for a small part of the population – the few who can afford them. From the beginning, IKEA has taken a different path. IKEA have decided to side with the many. That means responding to the home furnishing needs of people throughout the world. People with many different needs, tastes, dreams, aspirations... and wallets. People who want to improve their home and create a better everyday life. For IKEA, helping create a better everyday life means offering a wide range of home furnishings in IKEA stores. Home furnishings that combine good design, good function and good quality with prices so low that as many people as possible can afford them.

The brand name ONdigital was announced by BDB on 28 July 1998. On 28 September 1998 ONdigital revealed its programme and pricing line-up. Service commenced on 15 November 1998 less than 11 months after the licences were granted. ONdigital offers the simplest way to receive digital TV - through a conventional TV aerial (roof top or even set-top). In addition ONdigital offers customers the unique opportunity to select their own channels and, if they wish, to change some or all of them monthly at no charge. When it was launched ONdigital was broadcast through 22 transmitters throughout the UK. A further 59 are expected to be switched on in the next 12 months.

PLUG IN

PHONE UP

SIT BACK

digital

More choice through your aerial

No dish, no cable, simply an aerial.

Implementing corporate design

It is difficult to overstate the importance of corporate design manuals. They form the bedrock of corporate design, containing master artwork of the corporate mark, guidelines for its use, precise colour reference and even extensive detail in use of typefaces, grids and style of imagery. In paper, or increasingly – electronic format, they achieve unity in corporate look and feel by allowing a corporation to hire great designers once, and implementing their work everywhere.
They have the power to turn a single company representative with an aeroplane ticket and money into a 'regional presence'. The look and feel of every item of stationery, brochure, advertisement and sign will be identical to head office 10,000 miles away, if the design manual is adhered to.

Beyond manuals for just design, new media is reducing the cost, and easing the production of manuals for everything. The ubiquity of themed bars and restaurants points to one prosaic consequence of this tendency. Uniform high standards would seem to be a good thing, but we must remember that cultural diversity is the spice of life. This is a critical issue for all managers in major corporations. Ask yourself, did you contribute to improving the quality of the world, or did you homogenise diversity into a bland uniformity?

In nature, biological diversity is the prerequisite of rich and life-sustaining environments. The same must surely apply to cultural diversity. The warnings of attack from beautiful corporations apply here. If you have a chain of 300 identical restaurants, beware of the competitor who may succeed by emphasising in their advertising that all their branches are different. Although manuals are powerful, they are not a conversation. Head office dictates to the operating divisions. As such, they may be missing an opportunity to benefit from the diversity that may come from dialogue. The Body Shop describes how its global campaigning effort on political issues helps to refresh the dialogue between the global brand and local cultures.

McDonald's is happy to draw attention to the landmark buildings it owns. It will also emphasise exceptional design features where appropriate, but not without linking them to a bright, strong corporate signature. McDonald's will celebrate what has gone before within the frame of its own design style.

Corporate identity management

Identity management is of pivotal importance. It allows the corporation to be consistent and coherent, rather than fragmented, confused and disorganised. The following section looks in depth at the art of identity management, drawing on the experience of some of the leading practitioners in the field. Most of the comments are anonymous but they emanate from senior managers in a range of companies including Shell, British Airways, BT, Courtaulds, ICI, Eagle Star, Hays, National Power, Prudential Corporation and BP.

Identity management allows the corporation to be consistent and coherent.

Overall the problem can be summed up in a simple quote from a disheartened design manager: 'Our problem is that everyone can commission design, even the "backwoodsmen".'

British Airways has commented on how the design management department concerns itself with areas beyond simple visual appearance. For example, while making sure that a coffee cup used by customers bears the company mark in the correct colours and position, the department also considers whether it can be stored easily and used comfortably, if it is durable, etc. In this way, identity management becomes a form of total quality management.

Even after a rationalisation programme, a large company is likely to have at least four main divisions with perhaps more sub or service divisions operating alongside them. Each will want to develop its own distinct character. Striking the balance between the aims of divisional and the parent group's identity is an important part of an identity manager's job. A written design strategy will help to resolve such problems by establishing the aims of the identity and what it is supposed to cover.

Tone of voice is part of identity. The way complaints are managed, how call centres operate, the way the text on the Web site works – all these are all essential components in the communications mix. They are a defining characteristic of identity.

Identity managers may also have an increasing role in the development of advertising if they are responsible for ensuring that the corporations' core values are faithfully conveyed in any communication bearing the logo or logotype. In a monolithic organisation, any brand's relationship to the corporate identity will also be the responsibility of the identity manager. What this means in practical terms varies from company to company, but a simple example involves the use of the Johnson & Johnson Credo (see page 69).

The role of the corporate identity manager

If a company's corporate identity is to be managed with some of the techniques of research and analysis employed in FMCG (Fast Moving Consumer Goods) brand management, then considerable resources will need to be gathered in a single department. This is necessary because the corporate brand embraces so many different considerations: advertising; signage; internal and external communications; new media channels; human resources and recruitment; sponsorship policy etc.

The most clearly defined task for an identity manager is to ensure adherence to design guidelines. Any additional role will depend upon the brief – and resources of – the identity manager's department.

Tony Key, Head of Designed at BT from 1987 to 1995 has described his approach to the design programme as follows:

When I was offered the job, my first action was to undertake a large visual review involving hundreds of photographs. I photographed everything and said to the chairman: 'I can sort all this out for you but I will need two things: firstly a lot of money and secondly the full support of the board.'

Guidelines and manuals

Design guidelines must be on the corporate Intranet. From this fixed resource, individual elements can be made available to suppliers on a password-protected Web site, sent by ISDN or burnt on to CD-ROM. The key point is that the Intranet avoids the ridiculous expense of producing great printed manuals. The old-style printed manual was always a highly inefficient communication because most artwork has, since the late 1980s, been created in electronic form. Manuals have been used to convert these electronic files to print, and then the users would usually convert them back to electronic form. This was clearly a very poorly conceived process.

Design guidelines must be on the corporate Intranet.

One problem that is often encountered is the excessive freedom with which the logotype is used. If the design guidelines lay down only a few rules for application of the logo/logotype, too much diversity can soon enter into material produced. Identity managers are often being accused of 'stifling creativity'. But if design guidelines are sufficiently comprehensive, the identity manager will not need to make so many controversial and potentially unpopular decisions. Many identity managers have stated that their greatest ambition is to ensure that any communication from their company is so strongly and consistently branded that it can be recognised as being from them, from across the room.

Prior to the de-merger of Zeneca, ICI produced an innovative code of practice for use of trademarks. The main body of the brochure details correct and incorrect use of the corporate symbol from the corporate standpoint of the Trademarks Department, the 'ultimate guardian' of these symbols. The brochure was intended to be used in conjunction with the corporate identity manuals, and it helped to clarify the legal implications of design. In this way it added weight to the design programme that might otherwise be seen as an ephemeral matter of aesthetics.

One approach to raising awareness of identity used by many large companies involves producing broadsheets that outline the many varied applications of the corporate symbol, with a direct reference to the relevant design guidelines section appearing next to each photograph. These broadsheets are then 'stuck on walls' throughout the organisation – thereby helping to raise awareness of, and interest in, the identity design guidelines.

How to approach design projects

Many companies use a 'matrix' to help decide how to approach projects with the right resources. In one case, a company used an audit-level matrix that assesses which audiences have to be addressed. Using this system they reduced 112 publications down to 40.

Seniority can help push design projects along. A corporate communications manager at one financial services company oversees all design and advertising for this major international group. Some years ago he highlighted the need for a new identity. The company had many operations spread across the world with diverse and fragmented identities. He has enjoyed some tangible success in co-ordinating design and implementation over the last 10 years. His success has been assisted by holding a position of relative seniority within his company – working for an executive director and reporting directly to the chief executive.

To obtain the identity he approached a small design group, because he did not want to 'spend £500,000 on something I could not show the board'. Naturally, some others design managers would disagree with this decision. As a result of the new initiative, 32 different trading names were brought together under the new identity.

Establishing a network

One international company commented on how best to establish an effective 'network', considered to be the key to effective co-ordination, implementation and management of a new identity. At the time of the design consultancy's appointment, the chairman gathered together the chief executives of the operating companies and asked them to co-operate with the design consultancy during the research stage of the identity project. At the same time, the identity manager asked the chief executives to appoint project co-ordinators to oversee implementation.

In this way a network of implementation co-ordinators was set up with two essential characteristics. Firstly, they were appointed at a time when the chairman's commitment to the project was fresh in people's minds, and secondly the co-ordinators were appointed by the chief executives of each division, so clear lines of communication were established. Because the chairman of this company takes personal responsibility for external relations, the identity manager's department is well resourced and has authority.

Acquisitions and identity management

A large and acquisitive company described how the acquisition of businesses normally resulted in a demoralisation of staff. There is a natural reduction in entrepreneurial, 'frontier' spirit. The company was keen to stress that proprietors who sell their businesses receive excellent financial rewards, but in design terms there seems little to gain from forcing the fact of new ownership down employees' throats.

Over a period of time the new parent company logo begins to appear on stationery, literature, vehicles, etc. For more integrated businesses, seminars on design and communications are held internally. This diversified company does not strive to gain the advantages of monolithic identity through such methods as central buying. It does not have a central purchasing department, and there are only 15 people at head office.

This approach to design is typical of the loosely federated conglomerate. The key marketing decision that needs to be taken relates to the material cost of integrating and managing design, judged against the benefits of increased credibility in the eyes of customers.

The character of globalisation argues for strong movements in the direction of integration. Conversely, there may be a role for a more diversified and evolutionary identity strategy in the twenty-first century.

An identity manager spoke of the perennial difficulties encountered when trying to persuade divisions to implement a new design scheme. For example, faced with a new scheme a manager can say: 'My division is about production, we need to produce – it is the most important thing. Do you want me to put up these new signs, at great cost, and perhaps have to lay some people off as a result?' The identity manager should empathise and sympathise, but persist. Generally, operating companies 'hate the idea of being left behind', so they should be warned that the company is going somewhere – with or without them.

A major utility that has purchased businesses outside its core operations needs to be selective when applying the corporate identity to acquisitions. For example, for a business providing basic maintenance to households, endorsement from a reputable, established public company would be very valuable. Conversely, if a subsidiary manufactures consumer goods such as food, then association with a public utility might be seen as unappetising.

New-identity pitfalls

Extensive on-site testing of any potential design can help avoid trouble later. For example, British Airways discovered that their old logo – which looked like an arrow – can be confused with a directional symbol making it difficult or inappropriate to use on signage.

One company, when they implemented a new identity, did not know what to do with many thousands of old branded hard hats and Wellington boots. In the end the company sent them to Romania.

Some verbatim comments reveal a further range of problems and solutions:

- When we launched our new identity there were many questions relating to how far we should go with implementation. For example, should we replace signs on the main visitor routes only, or should we replace every tiny sign? We got a large signage company to do a complete audit of all our signs and they came up with proposals. The booklet describing the full range of signage was distributed to location managers and then they were left to implement the new design out of their own budgets. When applying the signs we had tight control. All the printed stickers or 'decals' for signs were produced by the same manufacturer.

- Forms are a nightmare. At the time of the identity review we managed to rationalise some 6,000 forms down to a few hundred.

- When the chairman launched the new identity, there was one divisional director who said 'I'm not having that!' The chairman said: 'You are a part of a team, and we are here to discuss what is best for the team.' The identity went through, and the director left.

Tony Key has commented:

We were getting ready to launch the identity when the leak happened. The front page of the Sun showed the new mark with a headline: 'BT blows millions on trumpet'. We just had to go with the launch from that day: we were bounced into it. It took three months for the bad publicity to die away. As a general rule I would say everyone who is developing a new identity fears a leak, but you must expect a leak.

It is said that the success of identity depends 90 per cent on communication. Perhaps the most important part of the identity design discipline is the regular, everyday task of design management.

The success of identity depends 90 per cent on communication.

Corporate identity launches

However, there are occasions when a new identity has to be launched. To give some ideas of how different companies have approached the task, consider the following three case studies.

Gala Clubs

The merger of Coral and Granada Bingo to create Gala Clubs resulted in a lengthy corporate identity design project followed by a spectacular identity launch. This launch provides a good example of how a high profile leisure conglomerate approached the potentially difficult task of enthusing staff and managers so they were excited at the prospect of change. Rufus Leonard managed the design project in conjunction with Interbrand.

Some 300 key managers from across the UK were invited to Central Television studios in Nottingham. Most were aware that a new identity was going to be launched, but few if any had any idea as to the new name and logo. Senior management felt it was critically important to maintain secrecy, so the surprise of the launch was an experience shared by employees of both companies in the merger, helping to bind them both in a shared experience.

To help ensure secrecy, some misinformation was distributed: deliberately misdirected faxes marked 'New Corporate Identity – Private and Confidential' were sent throughout the business. These featured a rejected design with a rejected name.

The business is about socialising and entertainment. In keeping with this aspect of the business, a 'showbiz'-style launch was chosen, based on a television news format. At the studios a large television screen showed the audience the television presenter Selina Scott reading the news. As she came to what was described as the 'final item', a curtain was raised revealing her sitting in the studios announcing the launch of the new organisation. Great emphasis was laid on the size of the combined venture.

The presentation included interviews on stage with the identity designer, Neil Svensen, and various company managers. Razzmatazz was added by a dance team who performed in the new uniforms with 12 giant flags in the new livery. In addition, 300 hand-finished launch 'packs' were distributed, each containing a beautifully boxed badge with the new logo, a further information sheet and a launch brochure. The whole launch cost £200,000.

The launch brochure provided the necessary background to the merger, but also helped to energise those who attended the occasion. It message to the troops was to go out and 'make it happen!'

Prudential Corporation

A former corporate identity manager of Prudential describes the launch of their new corporate identity in 1986:

A large theatre in London was hired for five days and 13 presentations were given to successive groups of people. About 7,500 took in the presentation at a cost of around £7-£10 per head. Twelve presentations were for staff but one was for VIPs and press (at £20 per head), to which competitors were also invited: our view was that as leaders in the industry our major identity programme should be seen as a very serious and deliberate occasion.

All employees of manager grade and above had to attend the presentations. Other tickets were distributed on a lottery basis to everyone – cleaners, post-room staff etc. Another 15,000 employees saw a video of the first presentation, which was shown during the same week. The objective was to motivate every member of staff.

External audiences were surprised to see such a campaign by an organisation of our stature. At the same time as the identity launch, Prudential began running advertisements that were rather different in character from before. This resulted in a lot of – generally favourable – publicity. We set up a separate press room so journalists could follow up questions and then ring their responses straight through.

To budget the launch, Prudential reviewed the project and asked: 'Is this a job on graphics or a statement on the company's position?'. A lot can be said but unless staff become energised by the launch exercise, nothing will change. It takes a lot of handling to prepare for a launch and people should appreciate that the press may be interested – don't treat them as enemies!

Financial services

The communications manager described the launch exercise as follows:

In terms of cost savings resulting from the identity, I can say categorically that they were considerable. It is hard to quantify exactly because the identity was rolled out over a period of time. One example I can give is that we reduced the number of letterheads in circulation from 32 to two, and one of those is for executive directors only. We were buying all literature centrally even before the new identity was introduced.

In terms of the launch and introduction of the identity, another reason for doing it on a phased basis was to make sure the directors here were happy to pay for it. If I had to cost the whole thing from the start they would never have approved it!

At the time of the launch we believed that an external launch would render us liable to flak. We informed relevant media but did not make a song and dance about it all. However, to the internal audience we made a big fuss. There was a glitzy launch in each European company.

Because we were having a phased implementation (running down stocks of old brochures rather than throwing them away), we felt it was vital to lock staff into the idea of the new identity. We had to make people want it by winning their hearts and minds. The way we made the thing an event was as follows.

We had to win their hearts and minds.

I had a live television broadcast connected to the top floor of the new building. Not everyone was happy about being in the new building so the identity launch served a dual purpose in introducing two new things. For the live broadcast by satellite to all our offices worldwide, the top floor of the building was converted into a television studio and cameras went through, floor by floor, until they reached the top.

At this point a well-made 20-minute video about corporate identity was broadcast followed by an address from the CEO.

Staff throughout the company stopped work at 4.00 p.m. on a Friday and watched the simultaneous broadcast on television screens on each floor at each location. For the first time ever, the company gave all its staff a glass of champagne. There was also a commemorative glass they could take away. The whole thing probably sounds expensive, but remember that we did not have to hire somewhere specially. We costed our launch at around £12 per head for 10,000 staff.

Monitoring identity

The task of an identity manager may be complicated by the independence of operating companies. This is why it is best to work to an agreed design plan. Otherwise, if head office is sometimes seen simply as an 'overhead', the regulation of identity may test the authority of the identity manager to the limits. Ideally, senior management should resolve the hierarchy of identity to provide a framework in which identity managers can operate effectively.

Many international companies believe there are considerable benefits to be reaped from maintaining regular contact between design managers across the home country and the world. Rather than all problems needing to be solved by head office, it is easier to recommend one person with a particular problem to another who has solved a similar problem. In addition, morale and overall interest in design issues can be raised through such networking.

One British Airways design manager has a novel way to ensure wayward departments improve on sub-standard design. Where something is sub-standard or otherwise 'off'-brand, the manager mischievously mentions the fault and then says, 'Isn't the chief executive visiting you next month?'. This will only work in a company where the chief executive has an interest in the quality of design and an eye for detail.

Shell International has a tradition of regularly undertaking reviews or audits of the corporate brand. This would involve the identity manager visiting many sites in a particular geographical territory and taking hundreds of photographs. These were then turned into slides and were submitted in an oral and written report to the directors of the business.

They were given six months to improve the quality of communications, signage etc. Failure to comply could result in the ultimate sanction – withdrawal of the right to use the trademark.

There are different techniques for gathering information about what is going on across an organisation. One method involves having 'moles' in various places who keep the identity manager abreast of things. This might be quite systematised or informal. For example, at Prudential Corporation, most literature used to be stored at one location, and every time a new item arrived a copy was sent to the identity manager by a 'mole' in the warehouse. In this way it is easy to see what is being produced. It is also very useful if all publications are numbered to assist the audit process.

A major retailer uses 'dummy' consumers who visit locations to monitor the degree of adherence to identity guidelines and also measure the level of service against agreed standards.

Many privatised public utilities have useful systems for managing design, loosely based on the bureaucracy of their state-controlled heritage. For example, typically there would be a central register of signs with grid references so they can all be found and reviewed easily.

A big problem with policing identity is monitoring those who think they are above it. For example, a manager of public affairs might commission a publication for MPs that looked dreadful and had nothing to do with the corporate design guidelines. This kind of error happens when managers feel they have a special reason to deviate from the corporate style.

The correct approach to a design project is often complex. It may be appropriate to assess projects against various criteria: is it for an internal or external audience? Is it corporate or divisional? By establishing the project's position within a design 'matrix', it may be easier to approach it with the right systems, budget and emphasis.

A great deal of time and effort could be saved if identity design and implementation guidelines took into consideration the diverse quality of contractors – the printers, sign painters, etc. – in different parts of the world. Complex combinations of colour or other design 'devices' may be beyond the potential of contractors in some countries.

Experience also suggests that the only way to discover what will go wrong in the application of a new design scheme to vehicles is to run a test with the real thing. No amount of research can compare to the practical experience gained from applying new livery to a car, lorry or aeroplane.

Desktop publishing is a constant threat to the integrity of corporate design. Inappropriate typefaces and other distractions can easily be produced and circulated. Some solutions to these problems range from having pre-set templates that cannot be changed, removing from computer networks all but approved typefaces and introducing publications management systems. Often there is too much promotional material. It may be possible to send interested parties some 20 or 30 brochures about the company, but not one that summarises 'the corporation'.

The regulation of identity involves persuasion. An identity manager needs both carrot and stick. As well as commenting to senior managers on how far individuals conform to identity guidelines, there are other ways to persuade. The identity department can offer to purchase some design from its own budget to show how a project should be approached. Alternatively, the identity managers may try to enhance the power of guidelines by denoting them 'quality standards' and incorporating them into a broader quality programme.

At one major retailer there is no formal corporate identity design manual, instead design is uniformly executed to a high standard because the company had a strong tradition of excellence in all its operations. This suggests that the attitude of staff to quality is as important as written guidelines, which can only specify how to enhance uniformity in communication and identity. Company induction programmes are important. New people need to be told about the company's aspirations rather than the company's depths.

One system for achieving conformity in design guidelines involves using a roster of approved design suppliers. If divisions are only permitted to use an authorised design supplier, and if they must always seek permission from the design manager before purchasing design, then it becomes easy to exercise central control.

Shell International has a design policy that has developed over time. Periodically, incremental changes (which the customer would never notice) are made to the core logo design, providing a framework for consistently 'fresh' design programmes that keep the communication and design audit channels open.

Key points in identity management

In summary, the task of identity management is:

- unglamorous
- under-resourced
- under-supported
- vital to the success of the corporate communications programme.

Remember, for identity management there are seven key tests:

1 Is the identity considered an asset?
2 Is the identity consistently applied?
3 Do you know what is happening?
4 Are you consulted?
5 Do you have an annual plan?
6 Are you considered as a resource or an obstacle?
7 Do you feel the identity is working?

CHAPTER FIVE

**The fundamental concepts of care
and a more holistic attitude towards business
practice will be the building blocks of success
for the twenty-first century corporation.**

TOWARDS A NEW BEAUTY:

SUSTAINABILITY
PRODUCT MARKETING

The fundamental concepts of care and a more holistic attitude towards business practice will be the building blocks of success for the twenty-first century corporation. Managers need to build simple, easy-to-implement strategies that achieve competitive corporate advantage by:

- recognising that without using care, business leaders will never build trust with employees or customers;
- acknowledging the environment and the sustainability crisis, while rejecting 'values-free' business strategies;
- acknowledging employees as humans not farm animals that give only in proportion to what they receive – so thinking in broader terms that the mere financial;
- acknowledging customers as intelligent beings, needing more than condescending, low quality or mundane communications, and desirous of rich experiences – they are searching for answers to complex problems;
- trying to raise the tone a little!

Life is too short for the volumes of banal consumption we are currently chalking up at accelerating speeds. The era of values-free, over-consumption capitalism with its cancerous vortex of 'work harder, buy more', is coming to an end. The successful twenty-first century manager will have to learn to migrate from the muzak economy of the shopping centre to the Mozart economy of mass customisation and a richer quality of life.

Marine life has suffered from industrialised slaughter

Attack of the beautiful corporations

The successful twenty-first century company will not sit idly by and allow ugly competitors to steal customers with the stale offer of lower prices. The beautiful companies will use all their communications – including design, advertising, tone of voice and ergonomics – to ensure customers and staff understand how entirely unacceptable the old, values-free businesses really are.

We should be outraged at the wilful mediocrity of the frightened managers of the post-Second World War period with their inhuman work-spaces and drab messages. We need to rally the troops to build a more beautiful world and profit justly from this exercise. Let us not forget that business is now, and probably will be forever, the dominant political force in society.

There is no need for a radical new philosophy. The requirements of sustainable development are simply extensions of the traditional demands of business. Unilever's partnership with WWF to prevent overfishing fits comfortably with the historical tradition of the company. The founder, Lord Leverhulme, had an attitude of prioritising security of supply, and this is now being applied in the modern context to protecting the sea. In packaging design and other forms of marketing, Unilever will leverage this alliance to win market share. The result will be good for Unilever – and good for the sea.

British Airways is converting itself into a truly global airline by trying to break down the stiff 'Britishness' of staff into a more engaging and positive conception of service. The strong but contrasting personalities of Nike and Diesel show how human sentiments like passion and irony can be effectively exploited by clothing companies.

The rigorous morality inherent in brand extension exemplified by Disney, and the radical anti-car stance of BT advertising in its 'why not change the way we work' campaign, are further examples of corporations behaving as positive agents.

Sustainability product marketing

Probably the greatest new challenge faced by business is the achievement of sustainable development. What does this much-used term actually mean? Within Shell, the commonly used definition comes from the Bruntland Commission, which states: 'Sustainable development means meeting the needs of the present without compromising the ability of future generations to meet their own needs.'

The greatest new challenge is the achievement of sustainable development.

To achieve this goal will require huge changes to the core business processes of most companies. Implementing these changes will be dependent on significant participation from consumers. Many goods will cost more, but others will probably cost less. Consumers will need to be persuaded that the changes are necessary. However, we are talking about ensuring the survival of their children, which is a powerful and instinctive incentive.

I describe the process of building new, deep relationships with consumers based on the demands of sustainable development as sustainability product marketing (SPM). The essential idea is as follows.

- The ecosystems that keep Earth safe for humans are quite robust – or else they would have failed by now.
- These ecosystems are in imminent danger of failing because various industrial systems have developed outputs that are so vast as to threaten nature's capacity to absorb toxins.
- The vast bulk of industrial systems are now controlled by the behaviour of free-market economies, which are causing such substantial impacts from industry that the biosphere itself is threatened.
- The demand for these resource-heavy products is so widespread and popular as to defy political action, for example as demonstrated by car use.
- Because they are so large, it is generally the case that substantial financial sums are being directed toward these unsustainable activities.
- Given that for every form of expenditure there is an alternative – and the larger the market, the greater the incentive to substitute – it follows that alternatives to unsustainable industries should promote themselves as such.

- In practical terms, this means advertisements should be created that absolutely terrify the general public. There are good reasons to be terrified, and the public should be told of the risks we face.
- Markets and advertising have been allowed to develop substantial and sophisticated mechanisms for allowing the public to select the best 'value' product in terms of price and quality. However, with the notable exception of cigarettes and asbestos, there has been little effort expended to limit or discourage damaging products.
- It will probably prove politically unacceptable for governments to deliver the bad news of the sustainability crisis to the public. However, it should not cost a government to allow, and even encourage, impactful advertising and marketing of products and services that increase the chances of human survival. Indeed, it is generally agreed by political thinkers of both the right and left that direct state intervention in the economy is undesirable. But to permit the full and proper exploitation of the market and marketing mechanisms for both the individual and common good is both acceptable and desirable.

- Many advertisers would absolutely love to get their hands on such incredibly powerful, meaningful product differentiation as is presented by sustainability issues. As 'unique selling points' go, the slogan: 'Danger, don't kill your children!' would have a huge impact and it should cause consumers to switch brands.

Reactions to this theory

I have some limited experience of communicating to business people this marketing approach. The two main reactions encountered can be summarised as rejection and a form of disempowerment.

Rejection, because there is a fairly deeply held opinion amongst many business people that matters to do with the environment are generally 'irritating distractions' from the main business of making money, and it is too difficult a step to contemplate how environmental issues might actually result in increased revenue.

Disempowerment, because even if a business person I meet agrees with the underlying philosophy, they usually say it would be an issue for the chief executive to address, and therefore beyond the scope of any individual manager.

Business and ecology

Why does business often ignore ecology issues? This is perhaps a result of a tendency that the alternative-economist Fritz Schumacher (1989) observed dates back to the birth of economics over 180 years ago. At that time the provost of Oriel College, Oxford, commented on his unhappiness with the admittance to the curriculum of economics: a science 'so prone to usurp the rest'. Has the false science of money perhaps risen like Frankenstein's monster to rule our world against our interests?

Business newspapers and other media have grown entirely shameless in extolling the twin virtues of 'aggressiveness' and 'focus' in the strategy and implementation of successful company managers. Whilst neither of these behaviours are necessarily incompatible with the approach to business set out above, they still currently reject the complex and innovative perspective that is required to harvest the substantial commercial opportunities resulting from the sustainability crisis.

Perhaps one can draw encouragement from the lack of ideological baggage carried by most modern corporate leaders, who are not always myopically focused on maximising returns to shareholders. And if any one company can show that the strategic methodology and approach described above works, then all will follow instantly.

There is, however, often a strongly felt, deep-seated and sometimes instantaneous rejection of any kind of business methodology that embraces or otherwise acknowledges environmental issues. This response most commonly emanates from people who, in my opinion, have a good understanding – or realisation at the unconscious level – of the irresponsible damage wrought by their own and most other companies. Such people breathe the 'values-free' oxygen of business indifference to responsibility issues and thereby prevent their conscience from 'suffocating' them.

The luxurious real or potential lifestyle of a successful or aspiring corporate executive is exceedingly difficult to give up, or jeopardise, through 'out-of-the-box' thinking. And this may be despite the fact that the board of directors often crave that kind of innovation and request it from their operating companies, even rewarding it wherever it can be found.

The polluter should pay for cleaning up

Corporate beauty is in the eye of the beholder

Even if they employ the greatest designers and communications experts in the world, hazardous companies will not look or be beautiful. More significantly, a truly beautiful corporation will attack them – and win. Beauty is the essence of sustainable competitive advantage. Over the long term, it is pro-life. For this process to work there needs to be a major increase in political awareness through advertising.

Beauty is the essence of sustainable competitive advantage.

As consumers in the marketplace wake up to issues of human survival and sustainable development by the good companies, the bad companies will suffer. There are many examples of good companies.

In 1997 I had the good fortune to be able to persuade Intel Corporation to invest in a small campaign to migrate people away from their cars and towards videoconferencing. The objective of the exercise was to prove that it was in the direct commercial interest of Intel Corporation to address the critical issue of climate change.

Cars and aeroplanes cause around one-third of CO_2 emissions and therefore make a significant contribution to global warming. Intel makes videophones and was looking for ever more demanding applications. Videoconferencing is particularly demanding, so there was in this case – as there will be in many others – a happy coincidence of interest.

I have heard numerous sincere environmentalists complain about the terrible danger posed by CO_2 emissions. In the same breath they exclaim that car and oil companies are too powerful to control. The only way effectively to combat a vast industrial grouping like cars and oil is to find a substitute industry. Computers and communications companies can substitute for 50 per cent or more of physical travel, while also improving quality of life. So it is both necessary and logical for computer and communications companies to use their vast marketing budgets to raise public awareness of both the problem of climate change, and the solution video communication offers. The computer and communications industries now have greater market capitalisation than cars or oil, so they have the power to do it.

The vital changes in behaviour required to avoid catastrophe will result in hundreds of billions of dollars of revenue migrating from the transport industries to the digital technology companies. As and when the largest marketing budgets come to bear we might, for example, see minute-long television advertisements, perhaps directed by Steven Spielberg, which will absolutely terrify us about the risk of global warming. The result will be a fall in car sales and a rise in expenditure on video communications. Science already informs us there is no choice. It is up to the marketing departments of digital communications companies to seize the opportunity. After all, we all want our children to survive, and enjoy half-decent lives.

The retailer B&Q in the UK has declared it will be 'carbon neutral' in the near future, either through the establishment of CO_2-absorbing tree assets or other means. The Co-operative Bank, UK, a pacesetter in the new discipline of ethical marketing, has already met and exceeded its CO_2-reduction targets under the terms of the Kyoto Protocol.

The Royal Dutch/Shell group of companies has both acknowledged climate change in numerous public communications and made a $500-million commitment to building a new 'fifth' division of the group, called Shell International Renewables. Although this investment is small in comparison to overall capital investment by the Shell group, it is a major positive step. Indeed, it should help manoeuvre Shell into the top five renewable energy companies, near rival BP.

It was John Browne, BP's chief executive, who was the first leader of a major oil company to acknowledge climate change as a serious issue. This could prove a pivotal advantage for BP's marketing in the years ahead.

In the words of Ron Somer, chairman of Deutsche Telekom: 'As we see it, our drive for success is not in conflict with our social responsibility, something we take extremely seriously' (1999). The company backs this up with innovative statements that translate in to classic examples of 'win-win' economics:

Modern telecommunications applications enable businesses to be run without the need for road or air travel. Greater prosperity without greater harm to the environment – this is only possible with consistent use of information and communications technology. Information is the only resource we have which can be expanded limitlessly and conveyed without harming the environment.

The only UK company to implement sustainability product marketing

The process of 'dematerialising' consumerism – moving discretionary purchases from toys to interactive games, from fashion to film – will be essential for sustainable development. For business strategists, think of this shift as relating to 'sunrise' and 'sunset' industries. How should your strategies change?

Annual reporting: the triple bottom line

There is currently a revolution in the way companies report on their performance. Peter Downing, a management consultant with Ottawa-based TG International Ltd has eloquently described this process as follows: 'Beyond the balance sheet and the bottom line, the worth of a corporation is reflected in its impact on the community and how it conducts its business with others.' He calls this sky-blue corporate social reporting.

The worth of a corporation is reflected in its impact on the community.

While a growing number of companies are coming to accept this principal, there needs to be a method to measure its impact on the way they do business. This is provided by 'triple-bottom-line' reporting. Triple-bottom-line reporting is the public accounting of a company's economic, environmental and social operating performances. It measures the wealth-producing capacity of a company for its key stakeholders.

Economic performance is, of course, accounted for in the company's financial statements, prepared in accordance with generally accepted accounting principles. But this is only one measure of the wealth-producing capacity of an enterprise. A second measure is annual environmental performance reports. To enhance their 'green' credibility with stakeholders, some companies are using the reporting formats of third-party environmental conventions, such as the Public Environmental Reporting Initiative and the Coalition for Environmentally Responsible Economics. In these reports, companies state their planned environmental policies and conservation targets, and then record their actual accomplishments. Companies that do not have environmentally sensitive operations have no compelling reasons to publish such reports.

A third measure is provided by annual social-impact reports. All businesses have social responsibilities and such reports provide an important assessment of the wealth-producing capacities of public companies in this regard. The new term 'sky blue' represents the scope and effectiveness of a company's social operating costs and benefits.

An acceptable sky-blue corporate report would consist of a stakeholder-benefits statement and a social performance report. The first statement would present a core of benefits gained by the company's stakeholders, comparing current year levels with the preceding year's, in areas such as:

- job levels – full-time, part-time and outsourcing;
- taxes paid by the company and by its employees;
- employee benefits – medical, pension, social care and profit-sharing;
- procurement – local, national, and international;
- community involvement – volunteering, grants and philanthropy;
- non-compliance penalties – fines and outstanding violations.

The social performance report would contain other pertinent information, regarding:

- the company's social operating policies;
- issues raised by social audits and actions taken;
- compliance to the company's code of ethics and business conduct;
- awards received by the company and its employees for their social actions.

It isn't easy being sky-blue, but it can be worth it.

A corporate social report can add to a company's competitive strengths – its financial stability, market share and corporate image – by communicating its sky-blue work ethic to its five traditional stakeholders (shareholders, employees, customers, suppliers and the community), as well as to three new and influential stakeholders (ethical consumers and industrial customers, human-rights vigilantes and rebel shareholders).

A corporate social report can also be a unique way to promote the company's culture to prospective board members. Moreover, the sky-blue work ethic could be the market differentiation with which to recruit and retain those highly prized stakeholders – skilled employees.

Corporate social reports can help ethical investors to judge a company's wealth-producing capacity in the global economy, particularly when management sensitivity to stakeholder demands is becoming increasingly important in order for the firm to maintain market share and to earn a decent profit. Such reports also enable boards of directors to deal with their rebel shareholders' causes.

Sky-blue corporate social reporting will soon be a benchmark of companies' success both at home and around the world.

Sky-blue corporate social reporting will soon be a benchmark of success.

Style, sustainability and the design industry

Designers and communications consultants often have both the privilege and responsibility to look ahead at up-and-coming developments that will affect their own and their clients' worlds. *Wallpaper* is a leading international magazine, which serves both the style conscious individual and professional designer. One of its founding editors, and a consultant for Wink Media, *Wallpaper*'s sister creative media company, Toni Spencer has spoken eloquently about both the necessity for creating a company identity and the

developing consciousness of sustainability and ethical issues in business and design.

She explains business identity in simple terms:

Within any business, regardless of size, you need to let people know you are there, what you're about and why you're more desirable than others in your field. To differentiate your company from your competitors, you have to create a unique marque. This can be achieved through simplicity and directness in approach and design, or the process may involve an innovative strategy or logo. To fulfil your potential you must always market yourself with your desired audience in mind. There's not much point in creating a fantastic website if your clients are traditional fishermen in the Outer Hebrides. You need to stimulate a potential client's interest, make them take notice but always make sure you can follow through with a sound product that lives up to its introduction.

Toni Spencer observes that for large international corporations, their identity can influence every aspect of how they work – from logo and interiors to how they treat their employees and in-house management structures. This unity is the essence of becoming a big brand and the efficiency and success that go along with it. There is however a danger that when taken to extremes this all-encompassing corporate identity can be detrimental to individuality and cultural identity. It would be better if these large companies could include – under a blanket corporate identity – separate sub-identities that better represent regional character. *Wallpaper*, for example, having started as an independent magazine run from the editor's dining room, is now part of Time Inc. and yet manages to retain much of its own unique character within a giant media conglomerate.

In contrast to a sometimes excessive branding of larger companies can be seen the lack of focus found in many smaller ones. What large companies have overdosed on, young ones often miss completely. As an editor in the design industry, Toni Spencer has had all too much experience of being approached by companies without an image of their product and a concise description of what they do, be it from an architect, company or young graduate. This often indicates a lack of awareness of their competitors and hence the amount of information sent daily to an international magazine. Immediate reference points and succinct presentation can at times be the make or break of winning the attention of the press.

Wallpaper has recently moved offices into a custom designed space. As a magazine devoted to design, travel, architecture and new innovation, the design of the office is intended to embrace these changes and allow the magazine to continue to inform the environment in the future. This process has revealed an important point: corporate identity should not be so prescriptive and restricting that it stifles the organic growth of a company. Toni Spencer believes the best companies do change and adapt, so you need a strong simple corporate identity around which the company can grow. In her opinion, less is more. Leave room for change.

As an individual, Toni Spencer's main interests lie in the arena of sustainability, and an issue that constantly arises for her is the gap of communication between this world and that of contemporary design. There is still a 'muesli' image that presides, an automatic assumption that eco design means recycled pallets, and fair-trade means Westernised ethnic giftware. Much of this is down to the corporate identity of companies and projects in this field. Some of the most fascinating technology and innovation exists in research into new materials, energy and communication. Many projects are related to enhancing contemporary lifestyles, and yet with the current style of marketing and identity, they remain marginalised. Frequently, wonderful new ethical and innovative companies are seriously undermined by poorly communicated identities.

Like many leading-edge observers of modern business, Toni Spencer is interested in companies that are modern, creative and sustainable. Those that are conscious of the 'social eco' of their product (a phrase created by John Bird of the Big Issue Foundation to summarise the social and ecological impacts of an action or product). She believes that the design industry, among others, is only slowly realising that it has to take responsibility for both its personal and business activities. In such a competitive market it is hard to take new issues, and the subsequent costs, into consideration, but progress is hindered further by the stereotypes still held about the green industries. These issues need to be made exciting and accessible and currently the information is not put forward in a form that is inspiring to the design and media industries.

Toni Spencer's goal is to initiate projects using her experience of the design world to create links between top designers, companies and colleges, and experts in the sustainable development and fair trade movements. An important element of this mission is changing the way these projects are presented to the public. By putting features about and news of this field into *Wallpaper*, seen as the ultimate in cutting edge and cool, she already has the process underway.

There can be no doubt that pioneering consciousness-raising by individuals based in opinion-forming organisations such as *Wallpaper* will accelerate development and awareness of the sustainability movement. A key organisation at the heart of this emerging new business paradigm is Social Venture Network Europe, whose headquarters are in the Netherlands.

Responsibility at IKEA

IKEA is a great example of an organisation that combines design excellence, a definitive corporate style and a positive attitude to the challenge of sustainable development. With over 150 stores in 28 countries, IKEA employs over 40,000 people with sales of more than $7 billion. It is a very unusual company. To quote the president of IKEA group, Anders Moberg:

The combination of good design, good function and low prices makes IKEA unique. We don't just produce and sell furniture; we also commit ourselves to reaching all those people in the world whose wallets are a little on the thin side. To stand on the same side as 'the many people' means being consistently cost-conscious throughout the whole process from product development and retail.

But it also means taking our responsibilities as a major international company seriously. Our customers shop with their hearts as well as their wallets. Increased awareness, responsibility and openness is good for everyone involved: for us at IKEA, for our suppliers and for our customers.

For us, the financial year 1997/98 was a successful one. Thanks to the help of our co-workers we were able to open new stores, enter new markets and achieve very good results in our existing markets. All of this gives us the opportunity to expand even further and thus come closer to realising our vision: not simply to be a home furnishing company, but to help create a better everyday life for many people.

When the company says it is for the many, that gives it an enormous challenge. It does not focus specifically on rich people and it is not in the market to maximise profits. The most important objective for IKEA is to expand to offer more of the world's people its products. This is a very unusual position for a company to adopt.

The product range is based strongly on the Swedish and Scandinavian tradition of home design: bright, accessible and functional. This follows the design tradition of great masters such as Carl Larsson. It is a style that fuses form, function and low price into democratic design, making design available for the many. The approach relates to both price and geographical spread. China and Russia are the latest targets for the company's expansion.

To be part of IKEA, employees need to feel that they share the values of the company. When they do share them it becomes possible to influence the company. This should make employees open, humble and mindful of the complexities of the world. Flexibility is embodied in the company's philosophy that anything is possible: if you want, you can.

Employees, or as IKEA prefers, co-workers, are informed of the underlying principles of the company in a small document written by Ingvar Kamprad, founder of IKEA, in 1976 called *The Testament of a Furniture Dealer.* The word testament in the title reveals something of the missionary zeal of the IKEA organisation and its spirit. It is translated into every language that IKEA co-workers use and is frequently referred to in discussions between staff and managers.

Some extracts from the document give a good idea of its content:

To create a better everyday life for the many people

Once and for all we have decided to side with the many. What is good for our customers is also good for us in the long run. This is an objective which entails responsibility.

In all countries and social systems, eastern as well as western, a disproportionately large part of all resources is used to satisfy a small part of the population. In our line of business for instance, too many new and beautifully designed products can be afforded by only a small group of better-off people. IKEA's aim is to change this situation.

Already after a little more than two decades of operation we believe we have had some success. A well-known industrialist/politician once said that IKEA has had a greater impact on the democratisation process than many political measures combined. We also think that our activities have inspired many of our competitors to work in the same direction. During the past two decades, IKEA has changed the face of the furniture industry in Sweden and, increasingly, throughout the world. Our revolutionary methods of design, manufacture, and distribution have made fine furniture available and affordable for the majority of people – for all those with limited budgets.

But we still have great ambitions. We know we can have an important effect on practically all markets. We know that in the future we may make a valuable contribution to the democratisation process at home and abroad. We know that larger stores provide us with new advantages on our home ground, while new markets allow for greater risk spreading. That is why it is our duty to expand.

The means to accomplish our objectives are characterised by unbiased approach, our different line, and our endeavour to relate simply and in a straightforward way to others and amongst ourselves. A better everyday life also means getting away from status and conventions –being freer and more at ease as human beings. It is our endeavour to become a concept also in this area, for our own pleasure and also as an inspiration to those around us. It is a question of freedom with responsibility, and here we demand much of ourselves.

No method is more effective than a good example.

No method is more effective than a good example.

Our contribution to the democratisation process, I stated before. To be on the safe side, I would like to add that by this we in no way take up a position concerning questions about equalisation of wages, for instance. You might say that we also want to tackle these problems from a different angle.

The following sections describe our product range and price philosophy which is the backbone of our work. Furthermore, we describe rules and methods which have become important cornerstones in the world of ideas which has made and will continue to make IKEA a unique company.

The product range – our identity
We shall offer a wide range of home furnishing items of good design and function, at prices so low that as many people as possible will be able to afford to but them.

Low price with a meaning
Most people have a limited financial means. To serve the many people, we must always maintain an extremely low price profile. But it must be low price with a meaning. We must not compromise on either function or technical quality.

No effort should be spared in keeping the low price profile. A substantial price distance from our competitors should always be kept, and we should be able to offer the lowest prices in every area of home furnishing. Within each product group there should be some 'breath-taking' items, but our range should never grow to jeopardise the price

profile. Low price with a meaning demands **much** from all of us. From the product developer, the designer, the purchaser, the administrator, the warehouse worker, the sales people – yes, from all cost units which can influence our purchase price and all other costs. Without low costs we will never accomplish our purpose.

Changes in our product policy
Our basic policy to serve the many of people can never be changed. Changes to the guidelines for the composition of our range, as indicated here, may only be made by joint decision of the boards of Ingka Holding B.V. and Inter IKEA Systems B.V.

To reach good results with small means
Waste of resources is one of humanity's most serious ailments. Many a modern building is more of a monument to human stupidity than a rational solution to a need. But small-scale waste is just as expensive.

To file paper you know will never be needed again. To devote time to proving you were right anyway. To postpone a question to a new meeting just because you don't want to take responsibility right now. To phone long distance when you might as well write a note or send a fax. The list is endless.

Use your resources the IKEA way. You will get good result with small means.

Simplicity is a virtue

Simplification is an honoured tradition with us.
Simple routines mean greater effectiveness.
Simplicity in our behaviour gives us strength.
Simplicity and humility characterise our relations
with each other, with our suppliers, and with our
customers. It is not only for cost reasons that we
avoid the luxury hotels. We don't need any flashy
cars, impressive titles, uniforms or other status
symbols. We rely on our own strength and our
own will!

To assume responsibility – a privilege

In every type of society and company and on
every level there are people who make their
own decisions instead of hiding behind others.
 People who dare to assume responsibility.
The more responsible people there are in a
company or society, the less red tape. Meetings
and endless group discussions are often a result
of the inability of a responsible person to make
a decision. Sometimes one puts the blame on
democracy or the need to consult with others.

To assume responsibility has nothing to do with
education, economy or position. Those willing
to assume responsibility are to be found on the
warehouse floor, among purchasers, sellers and
office staff, yes everywhere. And they are necessary
in all systems. They are important to every kind of
progress. They see to it that the machinery works.

In our IKEA family we want to keep the human
being in the centre, and to support each other.
We all have our rights but also our obligations.
Freedom with responsibility. Your initiatives and
mine, and our ability to assume responsibility
and make decisions are decisive.

The fear of making mistakes is the root of
bureaucracy and the enemy of all evolution.
No decision may claim to be the only right one.
It is the drive behind the decision which determines
its correctness. One must be allowed to make
mistakes. The mediocre person is negative and
wastes time to prove that he was not wrong.
The strong person is always positive and looks
forward. It is always the constructive people who
win. They are always a delight to others around
them and to themselves. But to win does not
always imply that somebody else must lose.
The most splendid victories are those where
there are no losers.

If somebody steals a model from us we do not bring
a lawsuit – because a lawsuit is always negative. We
solve the problem by making a new model which
will be even better.

Make use of your privilege – your right and
obligation to make decisions and assume
responsibility.

Most things still remain to be done.
A glorious future!
A feeling of having finished is an effective sleeping pill. A person who when they retires believes their contribution is over, declines fast. A company which considers its objectives accomplished stagnates quickly and loses its vitality.

Happiness is not to reach one's goal but to be on the way. Our glorious fate is to be at the very beginning. In all areas. Only by perpetually asking ourselves how what we do today can be done better tomorrow, can we make progress. A delight in exploring will take us forward in the future. The word impossible is and remains, absent from our dictionary. Experience is a word to be handled carefully.

Happiness is not to reach one's goal but to be on the way.

Experience is the drag on all evolution. Experience is used by many people as an excuse for not trying new ways. Still it is wise to rely on experience sometimes. In that case you should preferably rely on your own experience. It is often more valuable than long investigations.

The ambition to develop ourselves as human beings and in our work must remain high. The keyword is humility. Humility means so much to us in our work and for our leisure time. Yes, it is crucial to us as human beings. It does not only imply consideration and respect for our fellow beings but also kindness and generosity. Will and strength without humility often lead to conflict. Together with humility, will and strength are your secret weapons in the development of yourself as an individual and a fellow being.

Bear in mind that time is your most important asset. You can do much in ten minutes. Ten minutes gone are irretrievably lost. You can never get them back. Ten minutes are not the hourly wage divided by six. Ten minutes are a part of yourself. Split your life into ten-minute units and sacrifice as few as possible to futilities.

Most things still remain to be done. Let us grow to be a group of constructive fanatics, who with unwavering obstinacy, refuse to accept the impossible, the negative. What we want, we can and will do. Together. A glorious future!

Simplicity
A complicated word, because people have such a tendency to misunderstand it. It has nothing to do with turning the clock back, or avoiding computers and modern technology. It has nothing to do with scruffy clothes or untidy offices.

No, the key concepts behind simplicity are words like efficiency, common sense and doing what comes naturally. If we do what feels natural, we will avoid complicated solutions. The fewer the rules and the shorter the instructions, the easier and more natural it is to stick to them. The simpler the explanation, the easier it is to understand it and carry it out.

Only don't forget: no task is so 'simple' that it doesn't need explaining at all, and no one can possibly enjoy doing a job unless they understand properly why they're doing it.

The many people
We have decided to stand on the side of the majority of the people, which involves taking on more responsibility than might at first seem to be the case. Standing on the side of the majority of people means representing the interests of ordinary people, no matter whether that is good or bad for our own, short-term interests. It means getting rid of designs which are difficult and expensive to produce, even if they are easy to sell. It means refusing to sell in hard currency to consumers in countries with non-convertible currencies, even though that would make our profits bigger and our problems fewer.

Developing a range and presenting it in an imaginative, appealing way in all our stores demands a great deal of knowledge about the lives, hopes and aspirations of the majority of people. The best way to learn this is through personal experience, not as tourists gaping at things with our cameras slung round our necks. Using public transport is one good example of how to get nearer to people.

Our contribution to a better everyday life for the many of people means that rich and poor alike should be able to enjoy the benefits of a practical, pleasant home.

Think different
Daring to be different is one of the most important criteria behind IKEA's success. It is the thinking behind some of the most significant aspects of our business idea. Here are some examples. While other furniture retailers were selling manufacturer's models, IKEA started to design its own. While furniture dealers set up shop in the centre of town, IKEA was building large stores out of town. While others turned to furniture factories to help them make tables, IKEA got them made by door manufacturers. Whereas others sell their furniture assembled, IKEA gets the customers to assemble it themselves.

Never say never

If at first we don't succeed, we must try, and try again – until we have achieved what we set out to do. 'Never say never' is our motto. It describes our own special brand of positive obstinacy, perseverance, and that irrepressible determination we have to reach our goals, to ever refuse to give up. It's a motto which often comes in handy in the pioneering work we are constantly involved in as we enter one new country after another.

Status

A word like this, charged with emotion, is liable to be easily misunderstood. Literally, the word 'status' means 'position', and usually signifies one person's position in relation to others. At IKEA we claim that we don't need status symbols. What we really mean by that is that setting a good example should be the manager's most persuasive quality.

We are a low-cost company, and we must be seen to be one. Luxurious company cars, first class flights, separate dining rooms and washrooms for senior staff are all status symbols. It's not that we begrudge our hard-working managers a sense of status, it's just that status symbols like this don't fit in with our low-cost profile.

Setting a good example should be the manager's most persuasive quality.

Don't get us wrong. IKEA will reward its co-workers. There's nothing wrong with singing the praises of the people who make our company successful. No, this is a question of our credibility. Luxuries like this just don't fit in with the image IKEA has as a low-cost company. And, in much the same way, fancy titles don't do anything to help the image IKEA has of an unconventional, unorthodox organisation. Of course we want our key-people to become well-known – but because of what they do, not because of their visiting cards.

IKEA's corporate attitude

IKEA is almost entirely funded from retained profits. It focuses on what is most important and embraces a Darwinian approach to new store development with best practice from all previous stores making its way into each new one.

Part of the style of IKEA is therefore a very strong corporate identity, which is consistent all over the world. The same range is being sold worldwide. Each new store and country operation follows the same basic tried-and-tested formula. But IKEA is also a learning organisation, refining processes and best practice.

Although the corporate identity of IKEA is very strong, it is also necessary for the company to be a very responsive and listening organisation. In any country in which IKEA operates it needs to make sure the identity, company style and traditions are understood by people in that country, including all suppliers. Respect for national cultures is also important. The company recognises that it does not have all the answers, but by combining with the interests of the people in the countries in which it operates, IKEA can achieve tangible benefits.

To give an example of how this collaboration works in action, the IKEA design team does not operate in isolation from its offices in Sweden. Instead, suggestions for design are developed and carried with IKEA people on visits to suppliers. Then, in discussion with the suppliers' representatives, through factory visits, analysis of raw materials and production facilities, utilising what is best in each country, the optimum design process is developed. IKEA tries to manufacture in countries where the raw materials originate to avoid unnecessary transport. If suppliers suggest changes to the product that improve it, IKEA is happy. Such changes often result in the supplier charging a lower price. This is the style of the product development that IKEA uses to minimise waste.

In marketing, the company has a single, grand perspective. It aspires to a brand image that conveys trust. The name IKEA should suggest products that are good quality and low price – and that have been produced in a responsible way. From an environmental perspective, IKEA wishes to be recognised as sustainable with regard to raw material use, emissions during production and so forth. IKEA is symbolic of a small group of companies that is well prepared for the new consumer revolution – ready for the time in five or fifteen years when 'sustainable development' will be a phrase both recognised and understood by the majority of people worldwide.

IKEA wishes the trust it enjoys with its co-workers, customers and suppliers should be built on the IKEA name, and not be borrowed from other organisations. Rather than fostering specifically marketing trust, IKEA hopes it can achieve the feeling of trust from all dealings with the company. IKEA wants consumers to believe it is a basically 'good' company, so concentrates more on acting sustainably rather than marketing communications.

In the retail business, where there is direct contact between the consumer and provider, the importance of such trust in reputation is clear. For any retailer to enjoy success over the longer term there needs to be trust associated with the brand name.

Therefore IKEA believes transparency is important. Through such an approach trust and credibility can develop. IKEA believes it has nothing to hide and the company co-operated fully with me when writing this book. If IKEA develops a manual for educating co-workers in environmental issues or business social responsibility, or how the company relates to suppliers, it is happy that such documents are made publicly available.

Transparency is simply a realistic response to the sheer volume of information in the world. There will be material written about your company with or without your approval, so it is best to co-operate with the new communications environment and provide what information you can.

IKEA is an unusual company owned by a foundation. Because it does not distribute profits but instead uses them to fund expansion, it is able to plan in a very long-term way. IKEA does not have to prove to its shareholders or investors every quarter that the return on investment exceeds that of the preceding quarter.

IKEA can take a decision that, perhaps for ten years, it will not make profits in a particular area, but if the company really wants to be in that area, it can choose to do so. IKEA wants to learn from the Chinese retail market, so there are stores in Shanghai and Beijing. There is enormous potential in the markets of China and Russia, but analysis of normal key figures might suggest the stores would not be profitable. This does not stop IKEA.

IKEA does not believe its customers are necessarily aware or interested in its ownership structure. The company's focus in communication is on its products and how they can create a better home. It wants people to buy less expensive IKEA products and therefore have more disposable income. That is the approach IKEA wants to be known for.

IKEA thinks its role in society is no different from any company that wishes to have a long-term view of its development and its interests - with stakeholders, customers, suppliers and society. Building such long-term relationships also builds a kind of non-financial capital that can be used to develop and expand the company.

For IKEA the objective for people is to understand themselves. Why do you come to work? What role can you play in building a better world? How can you make a difference? Start from where you are as an individual and then find ways in your life to help you achieve. Corporations have values, but you need to feel that what you are doing comes from your heart: that is when you create credibility for yourself and your company. Then you can create capital out of relationships. This will facilitate the next step of development for your company – and for you as an individual.

What role can you play in building a better world?

IKEA has a very interesting attitude towards the alignment of corporate aims with the spirit and will of the individual. So, when recruiting in China, IKEA tries to find a way to explain itself to recruits who have very different traditions and preferences. Most Chinese people do now know Sweden or the traditions of IKEA. The challenge is to explain to potential co-workers in China not just why it is good to have a job, but also how to take part in the IKEA values and ideas. It is the company's responsibility to achieve the alignment of purpose by accommodating and enthusiasm.

The vast scale and scope of operations of IKEA, combined with its relentless ambition to expand, might make it seem a dangerous company. Perhaps it is reducing cultural diversity and undermining local industries. My view is that its commitment to non-financial values gives it great scope to solve more problems than it causes. And if we need big companies to solve big problems, I hope and believe IKEA will show leadership when it is needed.

CONCLUSION

Anyone in their thirties or older can remember when the communist leaders of the former Soviet Union, and their counterparts in the Chinese government, would wear a semi-military tunic instead of the modern two-piece business suit. That has now changed. Today the lounge suit is the universal attire for almost all male political leaders worldwide.

Similarly, the flags of many nations have a common look and feel. It is these traditions in dress and presentation that create the basis for consensus and conservatism. And these tendencies are all mutually reinforcing.

In another context, this process of 'concretisation' through process has been brilliantly described by Jonathan Miller. He observed that: 'Language bears the same relation to thought as legislation does to Parliament. It is a competence constantly bodying itself forth in a set of concrete performances.'

Looming catastrophes

But this process of acceleration in the speed of industrial development, combined with homogenisation and globalisation, is reducing the health of the world. Our political evolution has entered a period of systemic contraction.

Francis Fukuyama, in his book *The End of History and the Last Man*, (1992) has summoned up a fearful vision of our future:

The end of history will be a very sad time. The struggle for recognition, the willingness to risk one's life for a purely abstract goal, the worldwide ideological struggle that called forth daring, courage, imagination and idealism, will be replaced by economic calculation, the endless solving of technological problems, environmental concerns, and the satisfaction of sophisticated consumer demands.

At this point in history, I cannot believe the industrialised world is completely evil or wrong. Millions of people have worked very hard to build the incredible structures that support our lavish lifestyles. In many, many ways the achievements are magnificent. In terms of industrial development, the twentieth century was sublime. More than two billion people now enjoy electricity, telecommunications, safety, food, warmth, radio, television and unprecedented mobility.

Two looming catastrophes threaten this phenomenal achievement. Firstly, the sustainability crisis looms large. Climate change is top of the agenda today; something else will be tomorrow – if we survive. The machine of industrial consumption is too large for our finite spaceship Earth to support.

Secondly, exploitative trade permits human catastrophes to occur. Vast commercial power is exercised without responsibility. Traditional lifestyles have been disrupted to make way for the benefits of industrial production for the rich. But for more than two billion people these benefits have not arrived. They may never arrive. As the power of global corporations increases, there is real danger that the analysis of Karl Marx will come true.

In *The Communist Manifesto* Marx described eloquently the combination of capitalism and industrialisation:

It has agglomerated population, centralised means of production, and has concentrated property in a few hands. The necessary consequence of this was political centralisation. Independent, or but loosely connected, provinces with separate interests, laws, governments and systems of taxation, became lumped together into one nation, with one government, one code of laws, one national class-interest, one frontier and one customs-tariff… during its rule of scare one hundred years, [it] has created more massive and more colossal productive forces than all preceding generations together… a society that has conjured up such gigantic means of production and of exchange is like the sorcerer, who is no longer able to control the powers of the nether world whom he has called up by his spells.

This was written in 1872, but it could have been written yesterday. We have been here before. Although the Marxist dialectic has been utterly discredited – for, as Sir Karl Popper demonstrated in his book *The Open Society and its Enemies* (1974), you cannot predict the future – even so, Marx's analysis of unfettered capitalism should serve as a warning.

If Marx's vision seems far fetched, look at the global technology industry. The communications revolution belongs to the few winners, not the many losers. Ask yourself, what is your company actually worth? Microsoft, at time of writing, is valued at more than $500,000 million, about half the value of London. The wealth of the three richest men in the world is greater than that of the 48 poorest countries.

A beautiful future

It is time for our great corporations to evolve. As Bill Gates himself has observed, corporations now have a digital nervous system. They conduct, in his words, 'business at the speed of thought'. But it is not the brain that rules the world, but the heart. Corporations must develop compassion and empathy. Perhaps they must even learn to love.

Corporations must develop compassion and empathy.

Tim Cronin, president of Saatchi & Saatchi in New York, has said: 'Companies realise they're going to have to outmarket one another by reaching into a relationship' – by employing emotion in advertising.

Market mechanisms can allow this organisational 'humanity' to express itself, and thereby allow it to thrive. Through sustainability product marketing and cause-related marketing (CRM), the cynical companies will be ostracised. CRM can be seen everywhere from the Oxfam Visa card to the Divine Fair Trade chocolate bar. Many of us work too hard, for too many hours. And what do we have to show for it? Just drive through – or, if you dare, walk through – the poorest part of your city or town.

Rising stress levels are partially caused by rising prosperity. As well as working hard, we have to try and spend all that money, and spend it wisely. Edward Wilson of Harvard University calls this confusion of endless choice 'discontent with super abundance'. In the words of Richard Tomkins (*Financial Times*, 20 March 1999):

It is not more time we need: it is fewer desires. We need to switch off the cellphone and leave the children to play by themselves. We need to buy less, read less and travel less. We need to set boundaries for ourselves, or be doomed to mounting despair.

Managing happiness is the end-game of capitalism. Reducing demand for industrialised goods by considering sustainability or philanthropy is a commercial opportunity. And to be honest, there is something slightly worrying about the reduction of cultural diversity through global homogenisation. Human eclecticism can and will blossom to subvert the hegemony of regressive global brands. Corporations are now co-ordinating the world's consumption. Where material negligence or crass exploitation can be discerned, they will have to reckon with assault from their more beautiful competitors.

It is the beautiful corporations that will fight this good fight. And win!

REFERENCES

Authors: Barnet, Richard J. and Muller, Roland E.
Title: Global Reach, The Power of the
Multinational Corporation
Publisher: Simon & Schuster, New York (1974)

Authors: Bendell, J., Murphy, D.F. and Barrett, S.
Title: B&Q: From DIY Retailing to DIY Politics
Source: Case study prepared for the International Labour
Organisation (ILO) Conditions of Work Branch (1997)

Title: Learning through Partnership
Source: B&Q and WWF-UK (1997)

Title: How Green is My Hammer? B&Q's First
Environmental Review
Source: B&Q (1993)

Title: How Green is My Front Door? B&Q's Second
Environmental Review
Source: B&Q (1995)

Title: How Green is My Patio? B&Q's Third
Environmental Review
Source: B&Q (1998)

Title: Working Conditions in Developing Countries
Source: B&Q website (1 October 1999)
http://www.diy.co.uk/about_us/environment/au_
e_working_dev.jsp

Author: Churchill, Winston
Title: The Second World War
Publisher: Cassell, London (1949)

Author: de Geus, Arie
Title: The Living Company
Publisher: Nicholas Brealy Publishing, London (1999)

Title: Annual Review 1999
Source: Deutsche Telekom, Cebit (1999)

Title: Visions of Ethical Business
Publisher: Financial Times Professional Limited (1998)

Title: Stop the Chainstore Massacre
Source: Friends of the Earth, Press Release
(8 November 1991)

Title: Friends of the Earth Brings DIY Stores into Line
Source: Friends of the Earth, Press Release
(11 December 1991)

Author: Fukuyama, Francis
Title: The End of History and the Last Man
Publisher: Hamilton, London (1992)

Author: Gates, Bill
Title: Business at the Speed of Thought
Publisher: Penguin, London (1999)

Title: Making Sense of the Movement
Source: Green Magazine. Vol. 4, No. 7, April 1993
pp. 34-36

Author: Hodkinson, J.
Source: Speech at Forests for Life WWF 1995 Forest
Seminar, Stockholm, Sweden (23 May 1995)

Author: Jetter, M.
Title: B&Q Timber Purchasing Policy. Research
Working Paper
Publisher: New Consumer, Newcastle (1995)

Author: Keynes, John Maynard
Title: The General Theory of Employment,
Interest and Money
Publisher: Prometheus Books (1997)

Author: Knight, A.
Title: A Report on B&Q's 1995 Timber Target
and Business Partnerships: A Sustainable Model?
pp. 33-44
Publisher: The White Horse Press, Cambridge (1996)

Author: Knight, A.
Title: B&Q's Timber Policy Towards 1995:
A Review of Progress
Source: B&Q (1992)

Author: Korten, David
Title: When Corporations Rule the World
Publisher: Earthscan, London (1995)

Author: Lenin, V. I.
Title: Report of Eighth All Russia Congress of Soviets
Source: Council of People's Commissions (1920)

Author: Loewy, Raymond
Title: Industrial Design
Publisher: Fourth Estate, London (1988, c 1979)

Author: Lovelock, James
Title: Gaia - a new look at life on earth
Publisher: Oxford University Press (1987)

Author: Marx, Karl
Title: The Communist Manifesto
Publisher: Penguin Books, Harmondsworth,
Middlesex (1970)

Author: McIntosh, M., Leipziger, D., Jones, K. and
Coleman, G.
Title: Corporate Citizenship
Publisher: Financial Times Pitman Publishing,
London (1998)

Author: McLuhan, Marshall
Title: Understanding Media, the Extensions of Man
Publisher: MIT Press, Cambridge, Mass (1994)

Author: Murphy, D.F.
Title: DIY-WWF Alliance: Doing it Together for the
World's Forests, Research Working Paper, Corporate
Social Responsibility in Practice: Case Studies of UK-
based Companies
Publisher: School of Policy Studies, University of Bristol;
New Consumer, Newcastle

Authors: Murphy, D.F. and Bendell, J.
Title: In the Company of Partners: Business,
Environmental Groups and Sustainable Development
Post-Rio
Publisher:The Policy Press, Bristol

Author: Murphy, D.F.
Title: The Partnership Paradox: Business-NGO
Relations on Sustainable Development in the
International Policy Arena. Unpublished PhD thesis
Source: University of Bristol

Author: Orwell, George
Title: 1984
Publisher: Harcourt Brace, London (1949)

Author: Popper, Karl
Title: The Open Society and its Enemies
Publisher: Routledge, London (1974)

Author: Schumacher, Fritz
Title: Small is Beautiful
Publisher: Harper Collins (1989)

Title: The Shell Report 1999
Source: Shell International External Affairs,
London (1999)

Author: Frank, Thomas
Title: The Conquest of Cool, Business Culture,
Counter Culture and the Rise of Hip Consumerism
Publisher: University of Chicago Press, Chicago (1997)

Author: Wanamaker, John
Source: Advertising Age (20 March 1999)

Author: Weber, Max
Title: The Protestant Ethic and the Spirit of Capitalism
Publisher: Unwin, London (1976)

INDEX